How to get the job that's right for you

A career guide for the 80s

REVISED EDITION

How to get the job that's right for you
A career guide for the 80s

BENEDETTO GRECO

Dow Jones-Irwin
Homewood, Illinois 60430

ISBN 0-87094-194-1 (paperbound)
ISBN 0-87094-219-0 (hardbound)
Library of Congress Catalog Card No. 79–56085

Printed in the United States of America

1 2 3 4 5 6 7 8 9 0 K 7 6 5 4 3 2 1 0

Preface

This book was written to help you select the career that will provide you with achievement, satisfaction, and financial rewards.

The book is presented in three sections. Section One describes career strategy. You will encounter the theory in Chapter 2 and its application in Chapters 3, 4, 5, and 6. Develop a good understanding of this section before moving on to Section Two.

Section Two consists of Chapter 7. Whenever you find yourself dissatisfied with your current career position, reaffirm that you are in the right job for you by reviewing Chapters 1 through 6. If you are in the right job but your dissatisfaction persists, Chapter 7 will help you to answer the question, "Should I change jobs or stay in my present position?"

Section Three will acquaint you with the techniques of job search that get results. As you read with your job objective clearly defined, Chapters 8, 9, and 10 will assist you in getting the job that is right for you with a minimum of wasted effort and frustration.

Research and experience with professionals of all ages and stages of career development have prompted my writing. The concepts and techniques outlined in the following chapters will meet your needs in a lifetime of career decision making.

March 1980   BENEDETTO GRECO

v

Contents

Introduction:
Planning your career

Planning for a Career Is the Concept

Today's men and women are not thinking about a "job"; rather, their concern centers about the concept of a "career." The word *career* emphasizes concern for a long-range commitment to a profession which will provide self-satisfaction as well as filling the material needs of life. The appeal of professionalism in occupations is held with high regard.

The implications of choosing and managing a career which will cover a major portion of an individual's lifetime demand insight, planning, and preparation. The numerous cases of dissatisfied people who selected jobs without realizing the lack of long-range potential point out the results of poor planning. Their problem may have been a lack of exposure to many facets of the world of work, lack of varied experience, and a diversity of interests combined with limited knowledge about available career opportunities. Whatever the reason, better planning may have prevented their current state of career dissatisfaction. But who was there to offer useful planning assistance? Schools? Employer? Family?

Another concern, employers may not consider an individual for one of the company's openings if that person represents *turnover*. Turnover is defined as the acquiring and subsequent losing of employees.

Employers find employee turnover to be very costly; especially for highly responsible positions. An employer spends time and money in recruiting prospective employees. Additional time and money is spent in evaluating and hiring new employees. More time is invested in train-

1

ing. During the training and adjustment period, the new employee is drawing a salary; more dollars are spent. Company efficiency may suffer slightly during the training period if it becomes necessary to use the time of experienced, revenue-producing employees to train the new employee.

If the new employee resigns before becoming a revenue-producing employee, the employer has not only lost the dollars but also the time spent on the wrong person that could have been spent on another prospective employee. So the employer has lost what is passed and is committed to invest another equal sum to the next prospective employee. As a result, the growth of the company and company efficiency have been hindered. Employers, therefore, want to avoid turnover to avoid losing time, dollars, efficiency, and growth. And you can't blame them.

A major brokerage firm in the United States declares that they invest a minimum of $100,000 and 18 months in each new agent. The time and dollars go for recruiting, evaluating, salary, and training the new employee. The figure also reflects other inherent costs in new employee training and adaptation.

Turnover is costly and widespread. Employers are unwilling to invest their assets in a prospective employee who is not oriented, is unaware of the environment around them, and is not cognizant of what they are seeking in a career. That type of individual represents a high risk investment for an employer.

Regardless of your experience level, if you have not planned your career path, employers may see you as a high risk investment for them— you may appear to represent turnover. Turnover can be costly for you, too. Loss of time, dollars, achievement, and satisfaction are the prices you pay.

Change Complicates Planning

The problem in planning a meaningful career today is complicated by the vastly changing scope of activities around us. Statistics verify the fact that the fund of available knowledge is doubling every ten years!

A myriad of opportunities exist today that were undreamed of a few years ago. New industries are developing at a great rate. Along with this industry growth, new company-types precipitate new job functions which demand to be performed. Examples of change are numerous.

Technological change

Technological progress in the United States during the past 25 years is a dramatic example of change. Output, which is defined as the sum of goods and services divided by man-hours, has increased 3 percent each year for the last 25 years. Compound interest tables will show that 3 percent each year for 25 years results in output that has doubled in the last 25 years! No other country in the world can make that statement.

Technological change has made its impact upon all industries. In the field of agriculture, for example, there has been a decline of 200,000 jobs for unskilled workers every year for the last 20 years. Presently, only 3 million agricultural workers are feeding 205 million people in the United States; we still have a food surplus! In contrast, 75 percent of the labor force in China produce agricultural products.

We have not yet mentioned the introduction of the computer and its far-reaching capabilities and applications. Electronic data processing systems have revolutionized our offices and expanded our analytic abilities to an unbelievable degree. And, it's all just starting! Computers can even play ticktacktoe with you; the best you can do is to tie. Computers can also play checkers with you; after the third move, the machine has computed all the possible permutations of moves and you have lost.

In many cases, a whole new field of technology is brought to life to meet society's need. For example, we have a need for new sources of energy. An alternative to petroleum as our major source of energy because of declining reserves is being sought currently. Will the new atomic energy industry become dominant? Will the coal industry be resurrected?

Mechanization has resulted in more efficient manufacturing operations and eliminated blue collar jobs. Correspondingly, more white collar positions are being created. Back in 1954, the number of white collar workers surpassed the number of blue collar workers in our country. The trend toward services industries was begun.

Because of mechanization and high efficiency techniques the work week is shorter. However, the increased tension and pressure associated with the office job has caused a need for a new kind of service. Both psychiatrists and mental health clinics are in high demand. Sensitivity sessions and religious cults emerge to meet the needs of victims of emotional and mental stress. Recreation is used to fill time and to alleviate mental pressures. Golf, travel, theaters, spectator sports, hiking, and most recently tennis and bicycling are attracting dollars and customers. The camper-pickup and recreational vehicle industry is a major example of an industry which was created to meet the needs of a leisure-oriented society.

Industrial occupational change

Let us look at trends in occupational change. Blue collar workers are becoming fewer in number; the supply of white collar workers is increasing.

The United States is the only country in the world where the majority of the labor force produces services instead of goods. Approximately two thirds of our labor force provide services. Service organizations designed to keep society and its various mechanical devices working are increasing in number. Significant shift away from production employment is apparent because of increased automation.

Professional people outnumber skilled workers. Clerical workers and their professional counterparts (doctors, lawyers, teachers) account for 33 percent of our entire labor force. Clerical people alone account for 18 percent of our labor force; it is the fastest growing sector.

Demographic change

Changes in population location are clearly evident. Consider that the United States is composed of 50 states and the District of Columbia. Americans are free to shuffle themselves from area to area.

Today, one out of every six jobs exists in only three states: California, Texas, and Florida. One out of every $5 of disposable personal income is earned in these three states. Industries go to these three states because of available manpower; that is where the people are. Also, educational opportunities and facilities in these states are profuse.

Cities will continue to grow. Today more than 70 percent of our people live in cities; by the year 2000, 90 percent of our population will be living in cities.

Educational change

Everybody goes to school nowadays; *the average worker in the United States has more than a high school education.* Professional people have an average of 17 years of education.

Population change

Population in the United States is increasing! More than 205 million people reside within our boundaries. World population will continue to increase.

Age distribution is also changing. One out of every three people in the United States is under 15 years of age. This is due to the fact that the post-World War II girl babies are at prime childbearing age. The 1980s are seeing a shortage of people between the ages of 35 and 50. These figures are attributed to the low birthrate during the depression in the 1930s.

Women account for the largest increase in the labor force. Female participation has increased from about 32 percent in 1947 to nearly 50 percent in the late 1970s.

These figures combined with the facts brought forth in population change show a need to accelerate the career development of the young. The young are being called upon to fill the voids in middle management. Minorities and women are being sped into more responsible managerial positions in business because of their increasing numbers in population and in the labor force.

Population trends have significant influence upon our industrial development. An example is the baby boom which began in the 1940s and continued into the early 1950s. This huge increase in new population has presented a range of needs which greatly influenced our country's economic and industrial development. Let's trace its impact upon business growth and activity.

Because of the new births in the 1940s, baby food, baby furniture and clothing, toys, health and medical services, and other baby amenities industries blossomed into widespread demand. During the 1950s the education industry expanded to meet the huge demand for elementary and secondary education, and this brought about a need for more teachers and school buildings. A demand for youth-oriented health services also grew. As the children outgrew their parents' bedtime stories, outside entertainment vaulted into high demand as hobbies, live music, records, rock singers consumed countless leisure hours. As these kids became 16 years of age, they qualified for a driver's license. The teenager's need for mobility created a significant demand for rebuilt cars and hot rod parts since the cost of new cars was prohibitive.

As the 1960s came and these babies graduated from high school, they had been told repeatedly about the value of education and its role as a ticket to success and a productive life. Demand for colleges and universities with a corresponding increase in the need for teachers, buildings, and campuses was realized. Entertainment continued as an important need for the student population.

As this new population reached adulthood, they left their parents' homes which precipitated a need for housing. New apartments and low-cost houses were built at record rate. Furniture, home rebuilding and redecorating materials were in corresponding great demand.

The 1940s baby crop is now a group of college educated professionals, some with two and three degrees. Because of the rapid rate of change in our industries, these well-educated graduates realize a need for continued education through company training programs and special seminar programs. Their college degrees are found to be obsolete quickly; to keep up, they seek more training but not necessarily another degree. Therefore, a new era of education is being born; special seminar programs offering a wide range of topics are being offered by the colleges and universities which originally enrolled these customers on degree-oriented programs.

6

This same group of people is earning more than ever before. More disposable dollars are available for investments. The increasing complexity of insurance offerings, tax planning, the multitude of investment vehicles (stocks, bonds, mutual funds, real estate, mortgage investment trusts, real estate investment trusts, Keogh plans, commodity options, and syndications) has created the need for a financial planning service to help this affluent society.

As this population segment continues to mature, needs will surface such as: medical and dental services, gerontology research, retirement villages, and recreation activities for the elderly. Health services, government, education, and banking will be important industries in meeting our future needs.

National economic trends

Changes in the national economy influence occupational demand and thus job security to a very high degree. An important fact to realize is that fluctuations in economic trends do not uniformly affect all industries.

The following are examples of stable industries which are not radically influenced by economic fluctuations. Their demand goes on.

Baking	Finance and small loans	Photographic supplies
Banking	Food, canned and packaged	Public utilities
Cans and containers	Food chain stores	Shoes
Cereal foods	Glass products	Soaps
Chewing gum	Insurance	Soft drinks
Corn refiners	Law	Telephone
Cosmetics	Medical, dental and hospital	Textbooks
Dairy products	supplies	Tobacco
Drugs and pharmaceuticals	Natural gas	Variety chains
Education	Petroleum products	

More volatile industries such as jewelry, new automobiles, and the pleasure travel industries are the first to be influenced by a change in our economy's posture.

Change in you

Developing a career is also complicated by the fact that you change too. You are a dynamic system. Gaining experiences and additional education will promote change within you. As you mature, your values, needs, and abilities will develop and change. Marriage and children will probably change your financial needs and place more demands upon your time. As you achieve a "comfortable" level of income, salary will decline in importance. As you grow older, a sense of security and a record of achievement may rise to be your more important objectives.

Planning with Change

Planning is needed to achieve maximum personal development, but also to be able to present yourself to a prospective employer as a desirable employee. The major perceived complication to planning is change. Changes in you, changes in the available career opportunities, and changes in your relationship to a career are to be considered. The term *perceived complication* is used because no complication exists if you recognize the planning function to be a dynamic activity rather than a one-time, static process.

The planning system outlined in this book is an approach to career decision strategy which takes into account the dynamic nature of the bases for decision making. You will use it to direct your efforts, to monitor your progress, and to make your planning work for you as change occurs.

Many new industries will be created in the years ahead. Just as in the examples cited, industries and career opportunities will be precipitated to meet the needs and demands of mankind. Refuse to be intimidated by the scope of change around you; rather, accept it and use it as a positive force in your personal development.

section one

Career decision strategy

1 | *Put yourself in charge!*

One-Person Service Company

Have you ever wanted to have your own company?

Think of it! You would be the management in charge of an organization. You would be directing its operation, guiding its development, and planning its future. Your responsibilities would include determining the company's goals, designing the approach to be used in achieving those goals, and then managing the company's efforts accordingly.

If you ever wished that someday you would have your own company, your wish has come true!

You are a company! You're a one-person service company which is selling its services to a client called Employer. Your company requires competent management for it to survive and to flourish. *You* are that management. In this book, you will be applying proven business management techniques to make decisions and to manage your career.

Had you ever thought of yourself in this fashion? Every bit of management expertise you have gained through formal education or work experience can be applied to the task of managing your career. Consider the following analogies:

Business Function	*Corresponding Career Function*
Corporate planning	Determining the most rewarding career for you and the approach you will take to achieve it.
Marketing research	Conducting research and analysis to identify areas offering rewarding career opportunities.

12

| Advertising | Using a resume and other tools to notify employers of your ability to satisfy their needs. |
| Face-to-face selling | Using the job interview to convince an employer of your suitability for a position in the firm. |

Many more analogies will become apparent as we develop this concept. The important point to be made here is this: *You are in charge.* The skillful application of management principles to your personal resources will result in a career which develops as far and as fast as you choose.

Taking the initiative will be key to your career development. Regardless of the types of positions available, regardless of economic and employment trends, regardless of the many factors influencing career development, you will always find yourself in a highly desirable career position because you are in charge and are guiding your own career development instead of putting yourself in the hands of an employer. Because you are in charge, you will not have to wait for an employer to recognize your talents or for your boss to be promoted or fired before you get their job; you will know when to ask for a promotion, when to change jobs, and why.

You will know what factors and indicators to use in evaluating your career position at all times. Many companies offer absolutely no help to their employees to become more competent individuals and better qualified workers. The future of the company is considered foremost and exclusively; the future of the individual, the career development of the employee is seldom taken into account. Oftentimes a conflict of interests exists for an employer to tell employees that they are ready for a move and ready for responsibilities and opportunities that the employer cannot offer.

How many employees do you know who are waiting to be recognized or rewarded by their employer? How many who are just sitting, wringing their hands, wondering about what the employer is going to do with them? Those individuals are asking for continued uncertainty; they are leaving their future up to chance. They are betting and hoping that they will be part of the employer's plans for change. Is their bet a good one? Do they know the odds and the payoff?

But, the employer is not really a villain. The employer must be profit oriented or it will cease to exist; if some employees are not fitting in properly, what can they do? If the employer's rate of growth does not result in the new opportunities sought by the highly motivated, performing employees, should these highly desirable workers be told to leave? Many employers are doing what they can to help but . . . .

When you are in charge of your career development, your future is not in the hands of an organization which does not want and will not serve that responsibility. You won't be a tool; you'll be the craftsman.

Rather than an uncertain string of happenstances, your future will be a well-directed series of efforts making for a happy life and a sure success.

You recognize the need of a lifelong career management effort; deciding upon a presumably good direction for you and then burying your head in the sand will not be done. Because of today's rapid change in industrial makeup and in nationwide demand, deciding upon a lifelong career pursuit may be unrealistic. So managing your career to be sensitive to change will be mandatory. You will want to be ready to move; you will want to know when and where the opportunity exists.

To be in charge and to insure success, you will need decision-making skills. The ability to make the right decision at the right time is common to successful people in all categories of life. They may not make the right decision at all times, but they make the right decision more times than not. Habitual winners always seem to know how to evaluate a situation and how to base their decision upon an awareness of the important criteria. They know which questions to ask and what information is needed before making a decision.

How many people do you know who are in an unrewarding, unsatisfying career because they did not really know how to evaluate the company, the job, or the industry before they decided to take the job? These people are now faced with *frustration*.

Three alternatives exist to those who encounter frustration (see Figure 1–1):

a. Withdraw: Leave the job or the company or the career and start all over again in another area. If the skills of career decision making are not yet learned, this process will repeat itself over and over again: many jobs, many companies, many changes until the "right" combination is found. This may take a lifetime; in fact, the right situation may never be found.

b. Apathy: Stay in the job and forget about the dissatisfaction. Endure the situation, get the "Oh, I don't care" attitude; become apathetic. Assumption is made that "success wasn't meant to be for me."

c. Aggression: Aggression may be externalized in the form of active attacks upon people or things which may or may not relate to the source of the problem. When attacks are made upon people or things which do not relate to the source of the frustration, the action is termed displacement. The feeling may have been manifested when you heard yourself snap at your spouse after a bad day at work; he or she had nothing to do with causing your problem. Sometimes aggression is directed to an inanimate object. Consider what is really happening when you are swinging at the tennis ball or the golf ball on Saturday morning. Aggression may also be internalized. When that happens, hostility and resentment may come on the scene along with ulcers.

Figure 1-1
Frustration

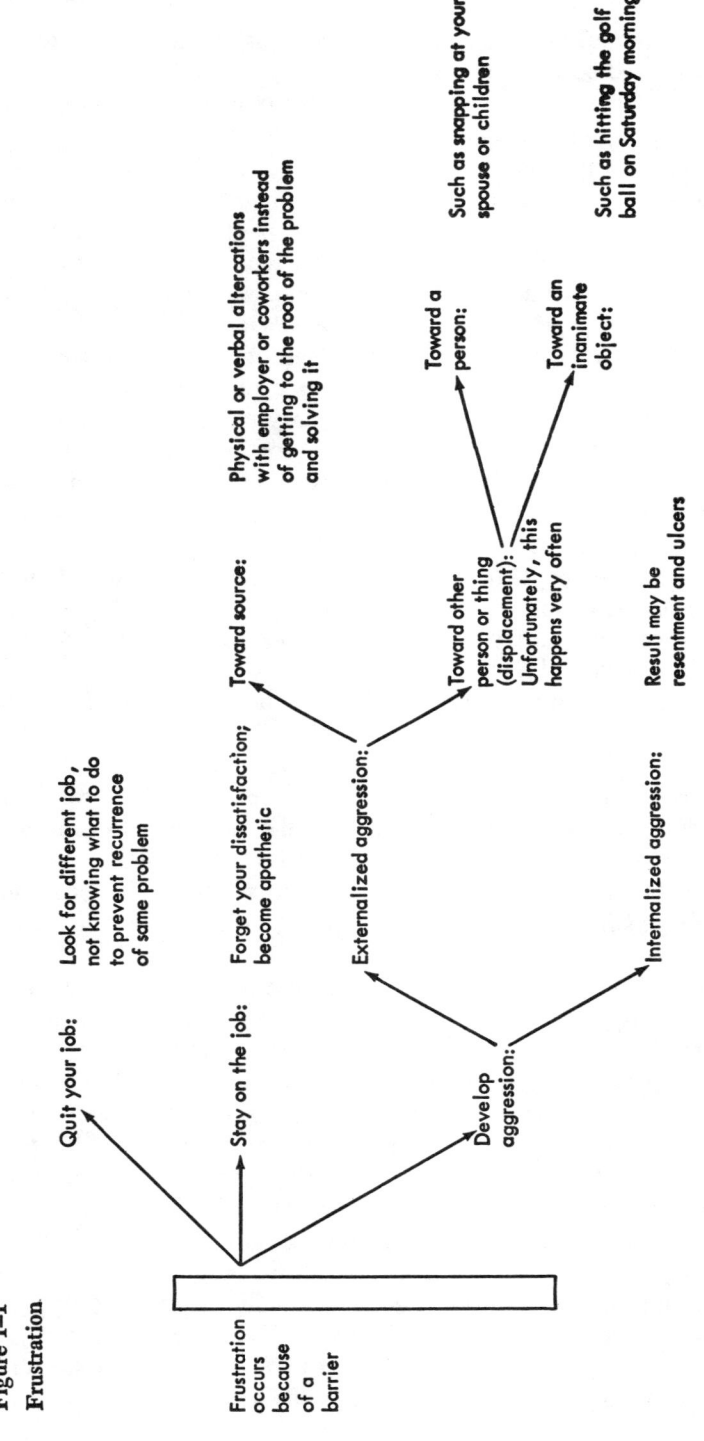

The three alternatives outlined are not attractive. Frustration is not attractive. Avoid it! Do not allow yourself to fall into frustrating predicaments.

Career Management Concepts

Prepare yourself for taking charge of your career by reviewing the following concepts:

You are ready to launch a career. You are going to be on this earth for a long, long time! Why not spend that time doing something you will really enjoy. Although the idea of lying by the pool, soaking in the sun, and making small talk with beautiful people sounds appealing—you'll want more out of life. Ask successful entrepreneurs what they like to do. The answer will probably be that they enjoy being productive; their approach toward productivity is their profession, their career. The word *career* emphasizes concern for a long-range commitment to a profession which will satisfy a full range of material, emotional, and intellectual needs. A successful career provides self-fulfillment.

You are thinking ahead—planning—thinking career.

You are the best qualified person to manage your career and you know it. You believe in yourself. Self-esteem is the foundation of high performance behavior. You are a capable and desirable individual who knows and wants the new and the challenging.

You are ready to take the responsibility for your personal development. Previous successes have been the results of your "taking charge" of the situation. You realize the importance of your being in charge.

You *can* and *want* to manage your career.

You want reliable information upon which to base a career decision. You have noticed every successful company president insists upon comprehensive, current information upon which to base decisions. Facts and figures and proof of their reliability are required before making any moves. You realize that the implications of choosing and managing a career which will cover the major portion of your lifetime demand information, effort, and planning. Lack of exposure to the many facets of the business and industrial world, lack of in-depth experience in a varied group of situations, and a diversity of interests combined with limited knowledge about available career opportunities are limiting your current ability to take charge.

You are ready to learn more, to take the necessary steps; you see it as an adventure, not a chore.

You realize that things change. You are not willing to stand still. You search constantly for more effective ways to grow and develop. You have observed that corporate management is sensitive to change. All corporations establish ongoing sources of new information; they also use that information in making their management decisions. Corporate progress is monitored through devices called quarterly and annual reports. You know that, like corporate management, the more you can learn about yourself, the better.

You will manage your career in a similar manner. Use a technique that will help you to be sensitive to change. You know that the ability to direct and cope with change will determine the degree of success to be achieved in your career. Seeking a long-range proposition such as a career is complicated by the fact that change is imminent in the environment all around. The facts outlined in the introduction portray a changing world. Further examples will continue to reinforce the fact that change is happening but, more significantly, at an increasingly faster rate than ever before.

You use a low-risk approach toward career decision making. You are ready and willing to take reasonable risks. But, you want to know how to calculate the risk. This is an important concept; and yet, it is sometimes forgotten even in the business world. The approach to decision making used by some businesses is to determine the product they will be making and selling. Then, look for a set of customers to whom they will sell their product. The questions they ask themselves are: What product will we make? and later, Where will we sell it? This process is backwards! Risk in this approach is incalculable; these businesses do not know if customers exist. Regardless of the quality of the product— if no customers exist, there is no business.

In today's complex world, the demand must be determined first. Then, *capabilities and personal resources* are used to come up with a product which will satisfy the demand. There is a great difference between *capabilities* and *product!* Capabilities can be used to make a wide range of different products; as demands change, those capabilities can be reapplied to make the different products needed to meet the changed customer demand. Risk can be determined more easily when using this approach.

However, those companies who do not understand their capabilities and instead see themselves as a product are greatly handicapped. As their market changes, the company may find itself without customers. Without the proper self-concept, flexibility is lost.

You also should strive for flexibility in your career design and pursuits. You know that capabilities and personal resources constitute the basis for many varied services. Those capabilities can be shaped and reshaped to allow you to fit into several fields and professions. But first, you need to research the market. What is in demand? What is needed? Then, your capabilities will be used to satisfy that demand or need.

You want to know where you are headed—at all times. Focusing your energies is the key to results and you know it. High performance people like yourself have a goal orientation in everything they do. Setting goals is not enough and you realize that. *Use* goals; use them to motivate and direct your behavior. Use goals to determine your actions and programs; make them work for you.

You have observed that when your energies are focused, your chances for success are maximized. You are more aware; you make better use of everything around you because their applicability to your objectives is more apparent. You want to know where your career is headed—*at all times.* All career decisions will be made in light of your career purpose. We will develop this in the next chapter.

Let us get on to putting you in charge. Remember, you are a one-person service company which is selling its services to a client called Employer. You are ready to build a plan.

Summary

You can create opportunity for the future by putting yourself in charge of your career.

Your initial commitment is to take full control of your actions and responsibility for your development. You never look to yourself or to others for excuses.

Performance is what you expect of yourself.

A well-designed, flexible, and yet definite plan will be used to guide your efforts. Concepts of career management will prepare you to build that plan.

How to develop a
career decision strategy

Career Decision Strategy

Where is your one-person service company going? How does it plan to get there? Your company needs an objective and a plan just as every successful company. Yes, every successful company has an objective and a plan which are very carefully derived through the following sequence of considerations:

a. What products or services are in demand these days? (The answer to this question identifies areas of opportunity.)
b. What resources (materials, machines, money, manpower) do we have at our disposal?
c. Which of the demands could we most effectively satisfy considering our resources and how will we go about it?

These considerations are made *in the order presented.* Companies find it most important that a demand for a product or service exists before entering the business. Demand represents *opportunity* to those who can meet it. Only after verifying that a recognizable amount of demand exists, decisions are made by reviewing the company's ability to meet the demand.

An example from the business world will illustrate the importance of these sequential considerations to effective decision making: A few years ago, a number of large established companies entered the field of educational technology. Two of the firms established a joint venture to enter the teaching machine business. Another firm established an educational division to produce and market training films and training materials. In the last ten years, many other firms have launched similar efforts to develop and market products for the educational technology business.

The decision to enter this business seemed reasonable because, certainly, a need to develop more educational efficiency exists. Current teaching methodology is not as efficient as is necessary to present the wealth of knowledge to our populace. Schools and universities are using centuries-old techniques which no longer meet our needs.

Another reason for the apparent wisdom of the decision is that we know that teaching machines and the innovative equipment and materials made available by technology can be utilized to update and revolutionize teaching in our public schools and universities. However, out of all the sophisticated, experienced companies who have entered the teaching machine business, none have found it profitable. Why?

The need is there, the product is there, but the *demand* is not there. There is nobody around to buy teaching machines. Locally elected school boards are the potential purchasers of this equipment. Unfortunately, they have a shortage of dollars to pay teacher salaries much less buy revolutionary new equipment which will take three to five years before changes and improvements in teaching methodology will be visible. In some cases, teachers are preventing the entrance of teaching machines into the classroom to protect their jobs.

The need is there, the product is there, but the demand is *not* there. Companies who failed to research the market before putting millions and millions of dollars and efforts into the venture found themselves in the middle of an economic disaster. It is not enough to manufacture a product for which you have capabilities or to manufacture it extremely well or to price it 10 percent below all other competition, you must also be sure that there is a demand for that product.

Using this approach reduces risk. Companies are insured against entering a business which has no customers and against entering a field where they have no capabilities.

As you notice, the concept is a straightforward one which you can use to insure that your one-person service company is always surrounded by opportunity. Let us be more specific. Here are the considerations you will make:

a. What employee services are in demand these days? (If you are achievement, action, and advancement oriented, you will concentrate on identifying growth-oriented industries and the demands they exhibit for employee services.)

b. What personal resources, skills, abilities do you possess?

Figure 2–1

Career decision strategy

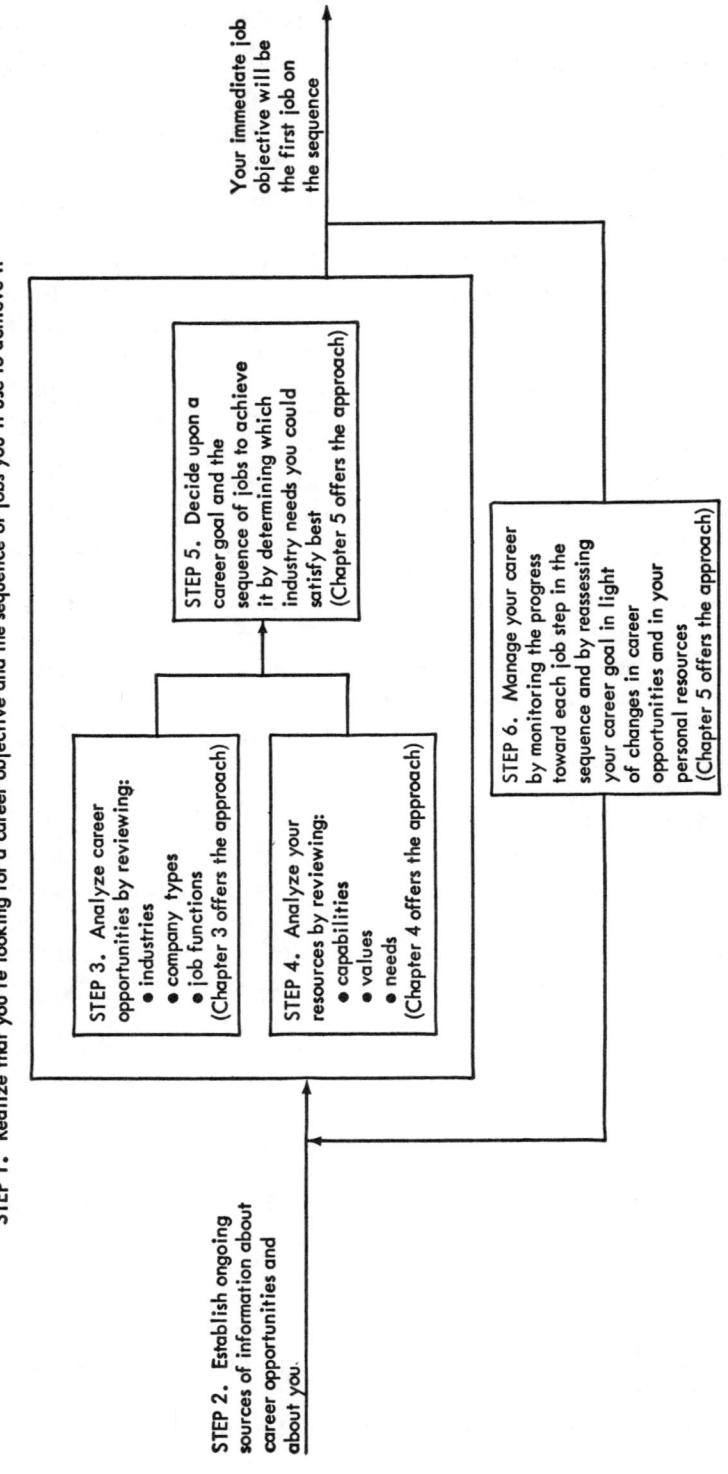

STEP 1. Realize that you're looking for a career objective and the sequence of jobs you'll use to achieve it

Your immediate job objective will be the first job on the sequence

STEP 5. Decide upon a career goal and the sequence of jobs to achieve it by determining which industry needs you could satisfy best (Chapter 5 offers the approach)

STEP 3. Analyze career opportunities by reviewing:
● industries
● company types
● job functions
(Chapter 3 offers the approach)

STEP 4. Analyze your resources by reviewing:
● capabilities
● values
● needs
(Chapter 4 offers the approach)

STEP 6. Manage your career by monitoring the progress toward each job step in the sequence and by reassessing your career goal in light of changes in career opportunities and in your personal resources (Chapter 5 offers the approach)

STEP 2. Establish ongoing sources of information about career opportunities and about you.

c. Which of the demands for employee services could you satisfy most effectively considering your personal resources?

Implementing the concept will be accomplished by the use of the six programmed steps of career decision strategy (Figure 2–1).

Step 1. State your objective in performing this exercise.

You will need to know which career you will be pursuing and which sequence of jobs and experiences will lead toward achievement of your career objective.

At this stage, the answers to these questions are not needed. The importance lies in the realization of the questions you are facing:

a. Which career should you be pursuing?
b. Which sequence of jobs will get you there?

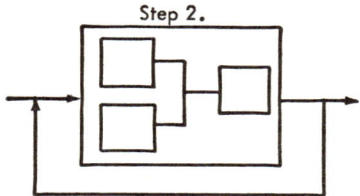

Step 2. Identify relevant information and establish ongoing information sources.

Information is the basis for decision making. But, what kinds of information will you need? Some of the factors you will bring to mind will be: growth of industries, availability of job openings, new types of companies, salary ranges, opportunity for growth and advancement, working conditions, benefits, job mobility, location, qualifications required, your educational level, your work experience and achievement record, the life style you prefer, the time you are willing to spend away from home, the salary you prefer, and so on. What else would you include?

Notice that the information required can be divided into two major classifications:

a. Career opportunities information (e.g., industries, companies, and job).
b. Personal resources information (e.g., your qualifications, experience, and preferences).

As you continue to compile this list of relevant factors, you will also notice that the information needed can be classified as ever-changing data. Managing your career means gathering and monitoring this changing information. Ongoing sources of timely, comprehensive, and accurate information are mandatory; effectiveness of the process will depend upon the accuracy and completeness of the data. Chances of arriving at the best possible career for you increase as input becomes more complete, objective, and reliable.

Where will you get the needed information? How can you keep it coming? Establish these practices as regular, ongoing sources of information throughout your working life. You need the information now for career selection and you need it later for career management and development.

Ask professional research groups for helpful information. Major banks and investment firms have large, well-staffed research departments who make a countless number of industry studies every year. Banks must be aware of the industry trends to enable them to make intelligent lending decisions. Similarly, investment firms and investment departments of large corporations must stay abreast of the business scene to insure that their investments are sound. Call the research departments of the major banks and investment firms in your area to determine the list of industries they have studied recently. Most organizations will provide you with access to their studies or mail a free copy for your use.

For example, the research department of a major California bank publishes a yearly study which forecasts the following: national economy, international financial picture, the California economy, California's major industries, California's metropolitan areas. Several times during the year, the same department releases reports such as: "The Retailing Industry in California," "The Apparel Industry in California," "California's Employment Trends," and "The Outlook for California—Its Industries and Trends."

Copies of similar reports are often made available to you—FREE. Just ask for them.

Establish a regular reading program

Daily newspapers (daily reading). Look for information about the economy, industries, and companies. Financial page is important; read it for industry data especially. Consider the Wall Street Journal as an important source of financial trend data and industry happenings.

Periodicals (weekly or monthly reading). Select periodicals such as *Time, Newsweek, Fortune,* and *Forbes,* which will offer coverage of a wide range of industries and articles of national scope. Use this source for tuning into the relationship between the economy and industries. Industry developments are sketched in many articles.

Textbooks (plan to read at least six each year). Read recent textbooks related to fields of your interest. Join a technical book club which will send regular notices of new texts relating to your profession. Call faculty members of nearby colleges to ask for titles of recent texts which have been reviewed and judged to be a positive contribution to the field.

Trade journals (monthly/quarterly/yearly). Identify and read the trade journals which treat your profession or industry. Specific information about companies, people, and new developments are offered regularly. See pages 124–25 for a list of trade journals by field; ask your librarian for a more complete bibliography.

Establish memberships and participate in professional programs

Professional associations. Become a member of associations related to your field or profession. Participation will allow you to meet and interface with leaders and influential individuals in your field, as well as provide a vital source of timely information. The library houses the *Encyclopedia of Associations,* an aid in learning the names and addresses of organizations which may be of interest to you. The table of contents of this volume is offered for your perusal on pages 120–21.

Civic organizations. Joining civic organizations will provide interface with people from a wide cross section of interests. Chambers of commerce, hospital volunteers, charities, political, and social groups sponsor programs of all types. Get involved.

Continued education programs. Continued education programs are growing in popularity across our nation because of the rapidity of change and development in every sector of the world of work. Formats vary. Evening courses, weekend seminars, and intensive, full-time, six-week training programs represent a small sampling of what is available. Topics and subject matter possibilities are literally unlimited. Call your nearest college or university for information about their current offerings. Participating in these programs will allow you to meet people with interests similar to yours.

Conventions and conferences. Attend as many as possible. Here, you can meet new people and hear new ideas regularly. This is the fodder you need to come up with new ideas for your career. Attend conventions outside your field too; broaden your knowledge base.

Learn to use the many references in the library. Appendix B offers a comprehensive bibliography of references, reports, and studies which offer industry information. This listing may be one of the most valuable tools you will use in your current task of career decision making, but also, it will serve you as a ready source of information in any job you are doing.

Don't overlook this appendix. You will find references like the Standard & Poor's *Industry Surveys.* These excellent studies, published annually, offer detailed overviews of each industry. Standard & Poor's supplements this information three times each year with updated analyses of industry and company developments. Industry surveys are published in all these fields:

Aerospace	Food processing 1	Liquor	Railroads
Air transport	Canners, meats,	Machinery, including	Retailing
Apparel—footwear	dairy products and	pollution controls	Retailing—food
Autos—auto parts	packaged foods	rail equipment	Rubber fabricating
Banking	Food processing 2	Metals—aluminum,	Soft drinks—candy
Building	Baking, milling	copper	Steel—coal
Canadian industries	and sugar	Metals—lead, zinc,	Telephone
Chemicals	Health care, drugs	gold, silver	Textile
Containers	and cosmetics	Office equipment	Tobacco
Electronics—	Home furnishings	Oil	Trucking
electrical	Insurance	Paper	Utilities—electric
Finance—small loans	Investment companies	Publishing	Utilities—gas
	Leisure time		

These studies are probably available in the business/economics section of your library. A plethora of similarly indispensable information is indexed in Appendix B. The information you are gathering now goes into a decision-making process made up by Step 3, Step 4, and Step 5. The process will outline the most profitable career pursuit for you.

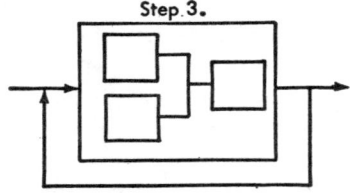

Step 3.

Step 3. Identify growth industries and their demand for employee services.

Begin your opportunity analyses at the highest level of cognizance—the industry level. You will want to invest your time and energies into identifying industries that are growing rapidly. A growth-oriented industry will be offering more opportunity. As the industry grows, new companies, new divisions, and new jobs will be created; additional talented people will be needed to fill the newly created slots. Here the word *industry* denotes a field of activity such as banking, insurance, aerospace, or agriculture. Within each industry are several company-types and within each company-type are several job functions.

The following list offers examples of industries which offered maximum opportunity during their time period.

1920s	Automobile
1930s	Radio
1940s	Television
1950s	Computer
1960s	Conglomerates
1970s	Service companies
1980s	?

People who had affiliated with these industries grew in responsibility and earnings at a much higher rate than did similarly qualified people in slower growing industries.

Once you have identified a growth industry, look for information about the company-types competing within the industry. Look for a company-type which is in the best position to capitalize upon industry trends. Then, identify the jobs which constitute the major activities of a company because these jobs will offer the fastest route to the top.

Ask questions about the people in top positions in these companies. Learn about their educational background and the sequence of jobs they have used to build their career. Identify the skills used in their profession and the means used to develop those skills. Inquire about the selection criteria used by employers to recognize desirable employees. But, remember, begin your analysis at the industry level; then, work down to the job level.

Knowing about a job opening does not help you to evaluate the field as a career. Unfortunately, most people begin their opportunity analysis at the bottom level—the job function level; they rarely ever bother to consider the industry or company-type levels. Consider the case of an accountant who is reviewing job offers from a public accounting firm and from a metals manufacturing company. The salary offers are very similar; the job titles are the same—Junior Accountant. Which offer should be selected?

One employer is a certified public accounting firm. The public accounting industry's continued growth is assured by the growth of businesses and by government legislation which require audits. The initial job assignment would be as an auditor, interfacing with 10 to 15 different companies each year. After three to five years, the individual would be promoted to audit manager. After five to eight years there would be a chance for a partnership in the firm where earnings may be at the $50,000-plus level. If, in the meantime, however, the individual becomes disenchanted with the CPA industry the accountant has met with and worked with the top management of 10 to 15 different companies each year; this network of industry contacts can provide job mobility. If the accountant decides to take a position with one of those companies, he or she had the opportunity to preview the new employer from the inside, thus providing a low-risk career step.

The other job offer is from a family-owned, small company which manufactures gears for a wide range of industrial uses. Demand for gears is predicted to be volatile over the next ten years; larger manufacturers will have the best competitive position. In this small company, four of the five company vice presidents are engineers. The fifth, vice president of finance, supervises the accounting activities. Opportunities for career growth for nonengineering personnel are limited. Most of the accounting assignments are in-house control functions. Activities will be relegated to company-designed practices. Also, the 33-year-old vice president of finance is the president's nephew.

If you were an accountant, which of the two jobs would you have taken? Knowing about the industry's trends and the company type is a crucial prerequisite to making a successful career decision.

You may be feeling a little intimidated at the scope of the task outlined in this step. Relax. What we have discussed here is the *gathering* of specialized knowledge not the *developing* of it. Knowledge is abundant; you can buy it, pick it up free, or have it brought to you. We will show you how to capitalize upon other people's specific knowledge about industries, company-types, and job functions to facilitate your career decision making. That's what you're gaining here—the concept that industry, company-type, and job function information do have a relevance to your task. The idea that these aspects of specific knowledge can and should be used in career decision making is my main message to you at this time. Later we will discuss combining specific knowledge with ideas to generate an organized plan—a tool you will use to achieve career success.

The specifics of conducting industry, company, and job research and analysis are outlined in Chapter 3. We offer a list of industries and sources of information about them. A comprehensive checklist to use in evaluating a specific company is also included.

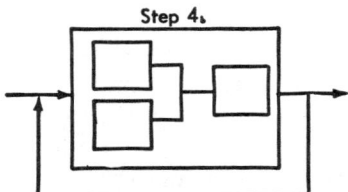

Step 4.

Step 4. Analyze your personal resources to identify your capabilities, values, and needs.

What type of information about your personal resources will be used in career decision making?

When you select a position which is aligned with your strongest *capabilities,* is in consonance with your *values,* and is satisfying to your *needs,* your potential for personal fulfillment and career satisfaction will be maximized. You'll like what you're doing. It'll be satisfying to you. And you'll be good at it! These three factors will be key determinants in career success; use these aspects of information as a basis for understanding you.

Some people cannot use this logical concept because they lack a realistic self-awareness. When they are asked about their abilities, they tell you about their college degrees or their job title. When asked about values, they reiterate religious proscriptions which were memorized at an early age (and abandoned as guides to life at about the same age). When asked about their needs, they quote their monthly cash commitments.

Idealized or misleading responses such as these do not provide the desired solid basis for decision making. You want understanding gained by reviewing facts. You want to know what abilities you have developed, not the names of your degrees and job titles. You want to know the values which actually guide your living. You want to understand your intellectual and emotional needs and their relationship to an occupation.

As the factual data about your personal resources is gathered, a feeling of confidence and self-assurance will accompany your sense of self-awareness. You'll know that you're in a powerful position and have the ability to make an accurate decision.

Analyzing your personal resources has prepared you for recognizing the types of positions you could successfully fill because you will know:

Which are your strongest capabilities and proof of that statement.

The specific values *you* seek in work or occupation.

Your particular needs to be satisfied through work or occupation.

The temperament/personality traits you will be bringing to your job.

My few words are offered in an attempt to impress you with the importance of having an *accurate* awareness of your resources. Upon this understanding, subsequent decisions will be based. If your understanding is wanting or if it is *misunderstanding*, all that you do in this process is for naught.

Your career will progress farther and faster when it is selected upon the basis of what is real in you. If all you have to offer at this time is a warm smile and a sincere handshake, admit it to yourself. This way, you'll know exactly what is needed and proceed to satisfy that need quickly and expeditiously. How much better off you are than those who have deceived themselves about their current resources! They will face failure after failure because of having based career decisions upon misleading information, and unfortunately, they'll blame outside forces for personal failures. Embittered individuals living a plastic life is then the result.

A handbook of questions is offered in Chapter 4 to assist you in cataloging information about your personal resources. The kinds of information you need, its relevance to work situations, and how that information is viewed by an employer are outlined.

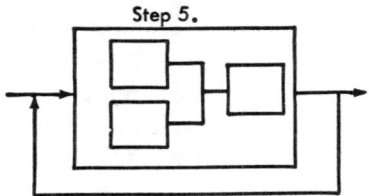

Step 5. Decide upon the best career for you and the approach you will use to achieve it by matching demands for employee services with your personal resources.

How do the managers of a successful company make decisions about a proposed venture? The answer is—they don't. They let the facts make the decisions. So will you.

As you perform the analysis in Step 3, facts about the most promising career opportunities will be uncovered. You will have identified two or three growth industries within your portion of the country and the names of companies competing within each industry. You will know why they grew, how they grew, and the factors which influence their future growth. The two or three companies who are in the most advantageous position to capitalize upon industry trends will also be known to you. Your inquiry will show the types of jobs available in these companies and which of them will be the fastest road to the top. Your research will have pointed out the requirements for each of these positions.

As you perform the analysis in Step 4, useful facts about your personal resources will be available to you. You will discover which of your capabilities is the most well developed; upon this capacity you can base your efforts for career success. You can judge occupational opportunities in light of their ability to satisfy your personal needs and to be in consonance with your values. You'll have that power because you'll have knowledge about and understand your values and needs and their relationship to careers.

In Step 5, you'll be matching facts, looking at the interrelations. Here, you will know which factors to consider and how to lay out your career. Because of your research, your decision will identify an achievable and personally rewarding career direction.

Unfortunately, many people start with a preconceived decision and then work backwards to justify their decision. Here is an example: You once heard that a good investment banker earns a salary of $400,000 each year. Immediately, you decide to become an investment banker (not just for the money, of course). Now, you conduct an analysis of the investment industry and of yourself seeking corroborating data to substantiate the desired answer. And you find it! Believe me, anything can be justified, somehow!

Another unfortunate situation surfaces when an individual makes a career decision based upon one of the relevant factors without considering its interrelationship with other factors. An individual may establish a career objective such as a sales person within an insurance firm. Yes, the financial services industry is projected to grow and prosper. Yes, it would be a fine career. However, the individual may not have the necessary capabilities and personal motivations to become a success in intangible sales. If personal resources are not considered in relation to industry trends in making the decision, the result may be an unrealizable career objective.

Another example: You may know someone who wants to go into teaching. His or her abilities, values, and needs are very closely aligned with the teaching profession. However, because of a declining birthrate, an increase in people moving out of the state, a decrease in people moving into the state, a reduction in government subsidies for education, a current oversupply of teachers, and a similarly bleak future, the choice holds much uncertainty.

Don't let that happen to you. Start with information and let the facts make the decision. Determine the best career for you by matching industry demands with your personal resources. Because of your research, you will know how to lay out the sequence of jobs which lead to the career goal you have selected; the first step on the path is your immediate job objective.

Chapter 5 outlines an easily followed approach toward:

Identifying your career objective in specific terms.

Defining a series of subordinate objectives which will lead to the achievement of the career objective.

Compiling an action plan for completing each subordinate objective.

Think of what you'll have when this step is completed!

You'll have a plan. You'll have a sound idea and the approach. You'll have determined the best possible career pursuit for you. You'll have identified the sequence of jobs and achievements which will lead to career success. You'll know how to qualify for those jobs and how to make progress toward each increment. You'll know that the career pursuit will be personally satisfying and rewarding to you. The structure and direction of your one-person service company will be defined. You'll be applying proven management and operations principles to achieve your objectives.

Why haven't you been able to apply business-like management to your career before? Perhaps you had no career plan before! Maybe, there was nothing to manage! No specific objective. No prescribed sequence of jobs and achievements to pursue. No well-defined, sound idea before.

When you complete the specifics of this plan and its documentation as outlined in Chapter 5, you'll have a *sound idea*. Your idea, your plan will require your management.

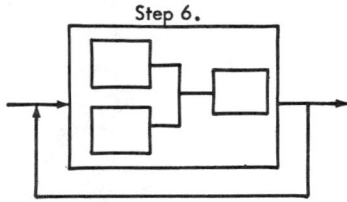

Step 6.

Step 6. Manage your career with feedback.

The approach outlined so far insures that you will always have immediate objectives upon which to focus your energies and efforts. The focus will mean *more results* and *faster results*. Having the plan is a great asset but that is not enough. Developing a plan is merely an exercise unless it's implemented and managed properly. Then, it becomes a useful tool. Use the plan; make it work for you by monitoring your progress toward the career objective.

Developing a feedback system will make the plan work for you in two ways. First, being provided with constant feedback enables you to react quickly, to refocus your efforts when needed. You can compare actual progress to planned progress for each of the sequence of jobs. You will be managing your career by objectives.

Second, a feedback system helps you to be aware of changes in our environment and in you. The career decision was based upon factors which represent dynamic, ever-changing systems; but you and career opportunities change regularly. As the factors change, the decision may need to change in order to remain the optimum career direction for you. If your abilities change because of additional education, if your needs change because of marriage and children, if industries change because of obsolescence, if company-types change as a result of new management techniques or new legislation—the decision must be reevaluated.

Establishing the feedback link will prepare you to manage your career because you will:

Be sensitive to changes in you.

Be sensitive to changes in the industry and company.

Know when to change or redirect your career.

Have the latest information about your profession.

Know which jobs are offering the most opportunity.

Be aware of whether your employer is keeping pace with the industry or lagging behind.

The specifics of using feedback reports to manage your career by objectives are outlined in Chapter 6.

Major advantages

The advantages of the six steps of career decision strategy are many. As you recap the process, as you review each of its steps independently, and as you consider it as a whole integrated process, its value will loom in magnitude. It offers you a precious commodity—Power.

Power is defined as organized and intelligently directed knowledge. The knowledge required to implement the process is, as you can plainly see, easily and realizably obtainable. Using these factors of knowledge in the proper combination will result in achieving the career success you seek. You will have the power to *Take charge of your career.*

You'll be able to direct your development because you'll know the factors which dictate development. You now realize how to use knowledge of industrial trends, company makeup, and job functions. You now realize how to use knowledge about yourself. You now understand how that knowledge can be organized to develop a career plan. The power to manage and to develop your career will be yours.

Along with the concept of power goes the fact that *your chances for success will be optimized because you will have direction at all times!* Focusing all your attention and efforts upon a specific goal will result in the highest potential for achieving that goal. If your energies were allocated to several different areas simultaneously, your effectiveness will be compromised. The difficulty which has neutralized efforts in the past is not the lack of desire to focus energies, but rather, it is the lack of a specific goal, the lack of *direction.*

The six-step process offers an approach toward gaining a sense of direction. It illuminates the factors that must be considered and the selection criteria which must be used to decide upon the most propitious career for you. Using this approach properly will assist you in arriving at the career where you will have the highest potential for success. As you change in maturity and experience, the feedback link will readjust your career objective offering a new sense of direction. However, at no time will you be without direction.

Summary

Your one-person service company needs an objective and a plan which will be determined by answering these questions:
    a. *What employee services are in demand?*
    b. *What personal resources do you possess?*
    c. *Which of the demands for employee services could you satisfy most effectively?*

The six steps of career decision strategy will be used to decide upon and manage the best career for you:

Step 1.   State your objective in performing this exercise.

Step 2.   Identify relevant information and establish ongoing information sources.

Step 3.   Identify growth industries and their demand for employee services.

Step 4.   Analyze your personal resources to identify your capabilities, values, and needs.

Step 5.   Decide upon the best career for you by matching demands for employee services with your personal resources.

Step 6.   Manage your career with feedback.

Major advantages of career decision strategy are: power and direction.

3 | *How to identify areas of* real *opportunity for your* career

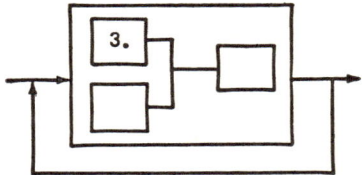

Go Shopping

What opportunities exist for your one-person service company? The key to career success and riches can be capsuled in this easily understood concept:

FIND A DEMAND AND SATISFY IT

Every successful business today is satisfying a demand. When the demand ceases to exist, so will the business.

You can learn what demands exist today. How will you gain that knowledge? Go shopping; discover what's happening. Caution! This does not mean running around town with a resume in your hand, asking about job openings. It does mean that you should gather information about industries, companies, and jobs being conducted. Shopping is a fun and valuable exercise.

My own experience should help you to understand the nature of the shopping expedition you need to undertake. Early in our marriage, I had trouble understanding my wife's definition of the word *shopping*. Sometimes I'd stay with our infant as my wife left early in the morning to go shopping. About six or seven hours later, she would return with a scarf or one blouse, the result of her day-long experience. As I went into a tirade about wasting time and the need for planning, she listened to my speech and then told me that I didn't understand.

I finally got the message one day when we were out shopping together. I spotted a very attractive dress being exhibited on a mannequin; the garment was on sale at 25 percent off. When I suggested to my wife that she should add it to her wardrobe, I learned my lesson. Her response, "Honey, that pastel peach colored print is last spring's; the latest stylish colors are rich greens and blues. The skirt is cut much too short; this season's dresses are cut about two or three inches longer. Also, the padded shoulders are out with this year's designers. Besides, the same dress is on sale at another store for 40 percent off."

How did she know all that? She goes shopping! You see, I thought that *shopping* was the same as *buying*. Not true. Shopping is actually researching and learning; buying comes later.

How to get started

You are probably wondering how to get started with this task. The list of industries seems endless; your group of interests seems diverse.

How about starting with your current employer and industry? If you have one or two or three other industries which are prominent in your list of interests, add those to your list. If you aren't thinking *industry* and instead have heard about a few job functions which sound interesting, start by asking which industries have that kind of job. Perhaps you can search through newspapers and identify these interesting jobs with specific companies. Then you can start by asking in which industry those companies compete.

Whether your interest was piqued by news about a company, a job, or a person, you must first identify and analyze the industry represented before being able to evaluate the position for you.

Figure 3-1 offers a list of industries which represent the majority of career opportunities in our country. Take your pencil and place a check by each area of interest to you. Then, find out about the career opportunities therein. Identify industries which are undergoing rapid change, have the potential to grow, and offer plenty of opportunity. Pinpoint the company types competing in the industry. Evaluate specific companies; determine which have the greatest chances for success.

A good place to start your research is a reference volume entitled, *U.S. Industrial Outlook with Projections to 1983*. Published yearly by the U.S. Department of Commerce, this volume offers brief (average, five pages) analyses of each of the industries represented in Figure 3-1.

Figure 3-1
Industry options

Aerospace

Apparel
Men's and boy's outerwear
Women's and misses' outerwear
Girls' and children's outerwear

Banking and securities
Commercial banking
Securities

Beverages
Malt liquors
Soft drinks

Building materials
Concrete and cement
Plumbing and heating equipment
Fabricated structural steel

Business machines
Electronic computing equipment

Chemicals and allied products
Industrial inorganic chemicals
Industrial organic chemicals
Plastics materials and resins
Drugs and pharmaceuticals
Soaps, detergents, and cleaning compounds
Cosmetics and toilet preparations
Paints and allied products

Communications
Domestic telephone and telegraph
International telephone and telegraph
Radio broadcasting
Television broadcasting

Construction

Containers and packaging
Folding paper boxes
Fiber boxes
Glass containers
Metal cans
Metal shipping containers

Educational services

Electrical transmission, distribution and industrial equipment
Power distribution and specialty transformers

Electronic equipment and components
Consumer electronics
Telephone and telegraph equipment
Electronic systems and equipment
Electronic components

Franchising

Food
Meat and poultry products
Fruits and vegetables
Confectionery products

General components
Valves and pipefittings
Ball and roller bearings

General industrial machinery
Materials handling equipment
Pumps and compressors
Air conditioning and commercial and industrial refrigeration

Health and medical services

Household consumer durables
Household appliances
Household furniture

Instruments for measurement, analysis, and control
Electrical measuring instruments
Laboratory and engineering instruments
Measuring and controlling instruments
Automatic temperature controls
Optical instruments and lenses

Insurance
Life insurance
Property and liability insurance

Leather and leather products
Leather tanning and finishing
Shoes and slippers
Luggage and personal leather goods

Figure 3–1 (continued)

Lighting and wiring equipment
Electric lamps (bulbs)
Lighting fixtures

Lumber and wood products
Lumber
Soft plywood

Man-made fibers

Medical and dental instruments and supplies

Metalworking machinery
Machine tools
Metal-cutting tools
Tool and die products
Welding equipment

Mobile homes

Motor vehicles
Automobiles
Truck and bus chassis
Truck and bus bodies
Truck trailers

Paper and board
Sanitary paper products

Personal consumer durables
Jewelry
Toys, games, dolls, and children's vehicles
Sporting and athletic goods

Photographic equipment and supplies

Pollution abatement equipment

Power equipment
Power boilers and nuclear reactors
Engines and turbines, steam, hydraulic and gas
Industrial internal combustion engines

Primary metals
Ferrous castings
Steel
Aluminum
Copper

Printing and publishing
Newspapers
Periodicals
Book publishing
Book printing
Commercial printing
Manifold business forms
Typesetting

Retail trade
Department stores
Variety stores
Drug stores
Apparel stores
Restaurants and bars
Grocery stores

Rubber and plastics products
Synthetic rubber
Tires and inner tubes

Selected Services
Hotels and motels
Advertising agencies
Automobile services
Motion pictures

Shipbuilding and repair

Special industry machinery
Farm machinery
Construction machinery
Mining machinery
Oil field machinery
Food products machinery
Textile machinery
Printing machinery

Textile mill products
Spun yarns
Broadwoven fabrics

Tobacco

Transportation
Airline
Railroading
Shipping
Trucking
Wholesale trade

Problems, trends, and potential of each industry are discussed and presented in a straightforward, objective manner. It is available for review in most libraries and is sold in federal bookstores ($8.75). It may also be purchased by writing to: Superintendent of Documents, U.S. Government Printing Office, Washington, D.C. 20402.

The initial handicap will be your inability to evaluate what you read and see. What basis will you use to judge the information you gather? This chapter is designed to offer a framework for investigation; the following three sections will explain how to use this information to understand industries, company types, and prospective employers.

As you consider a profession, an employer, or a field, look for demand; *begin your research at the highest level of cognizance and proceed in steps of increasing detail. Start with industry research, proceed to the company types within the industry, and then to the company itself.* Understand the industry's potential for growth and the factors which determine the industry's chances for success. If the future of the industry looks poor, investigate another industry, and another until you identify one with potential. Then, review the types of companies currently competing in the industry; determine which are leading and why. Identify those best equipped to cope with future trends in the industry. Finally, we'll see how to evaluate a specific company in light of your career aspirations; we'll assess the employer's ability to complement your personal development. Let's start with the type of information you will need to evaluate an industry.

I. Industry Selection

It's easier and more profitable to join a prosperous, dynamic, fast-growing industry than to affiliate with a staid or declining industry. In an industry which is enjoying growth and expansion, opportunities for rapid advancement and personal development will be more profuse. As companies grow in size and numbers within the industry, new job opportunities will become available; many promotions will be necessary. Industry trends can greatly influence career growth potential. Here is an illustration.

In the 1960s, the electronic data processing (EDP) industry grew at an incredible rate. Competent manpower was needed. During these years, young inexperienced college graduates were snapped up, trained quickly (and well), and put out selling computers and computer software systems. The companies grew so large and so fast that every competent employee realized astronomical career and salary growth. Some young employers found themselves to be district and area sales managers or senior systems engineering managers after only three- or four-years' experience.

Many of the 1970 college graduates who had the same education and potential as their school's recent alumni also took jobs in the EDP industry. In 1973, they were still staff engineers or salesmen instead of district and area managers. Why?

The industry's rapid growth had slowed. Also, the industry had now developed a large team of well-experienced and relatively young managers. The new jobs which had become available in the past due to company expansion no longer continued to materialize. Now, the only openings available are the results of employee attrition. The EDP industry's manpower needs, its growth rate, and the opportunity offered are now very different from a few years ago.

Use the following outline to aid you in identifying relevant data about each industry of interest. When you've unearthed the answers to these questions, you'll know the industry.

1. Influence of population, economy, legislation, and technology upon the industry. When reviewing an industry as you consider it as a spot for building your career, ask the following questions:

a. Are *population trends* influencing the industry's development?
b. Does the *national economy* have significant influence over the well-being of the industry?
c. Will recent or pending *legislation* open new opportunities for the industry?
d. What new *technological developments* may influence the future of the industry?

2. Industry background—nationally and in the geographic area of interest. Here, you will want to know the factors which caused the industry to be born. Determine the approach used by the industry to get started and to flourish. You will also want to learn about the industry's degree of success in meeting the changing needs of our environment.

a. What background trends have been exhibited in industry growth? What caused it to grow?
b. What has been the impact of social and environmental changes upon the industry?
c. Have industry profits grown correspondingly with industry activity in the past? Have losses been recorded by many companies within the industry? What factors caused the losses?

3. Present general trends and business patterns within the industry. Evaluate the match between today's needs and the industry's ability to satisfy those needs. You will want to know if the industry is rapidly becoming obsolete; discover the techniques being used to keep pace.

a. What have been the *latest trends* in industry growth?
b. Does the industry have competition from other industries?

c. What portion of the industry comprises the greatest source of profits?

d. What markets does the industry currently serve?

4. Problems of the industry. The four M's (manpower, materials, money, and machines) are the vital components of the major industries. Consider the supply and condition of each M in the industry being studied. Be sure that future supplies of each will be available.

a. Do problems with labor unions exist? Is the supply of labor sufficient?

b. Is the supply of raw materials plentiful?

c. Are the machines and equipment necessary for industry growth available?

d. Is the financing required for continued operation available?

5. Federal government's impact upon the industry. The aerospace industry which employed hundreds of thousands of men and women and accounted for billions of dollars in industrial activity is an example of an industry which is closely dependent upon the federal government's spending. Understand the relationship between our government's activities and the growth and development of the industry of your choice.

a. Will recent or pending legislation restrict industry activity?

b. Do federal, state or local governmental spending activities have direct influence upon industry growth?

6. Future trends within the industry. Knowing the industry's plans for the future will help you to identify areas of greatest importance and areas of greatest *opportunity* within the industry. Also, this knowledge will prevent you from affiliating with a seemingly healthy area which will soon be deemphasized.

a. Is the industry planning to penetrate additional market segments? Do plans exist for offering additional products and services to existing markets?

b. Does the industry plan vertical or horizontal growth?

c. Are new sources of financing being explored? Are new techniques of financing being considered?

II. How to Compare and Contrast Company Types

Once you have identified a promising industry, you will want to know which company-type will be in the best competitive position to capitalize upon industry trends. Consider the restaurant industry as an illustration. Within the industry are several company types:

a. Elegant dining establishments (evening meals only). Complete menu of epicurean delights, table cloths, silver, china, waiters, waitresses, wine stewards, parking attendants, experienced European-born chefs, and well-trained kitchen staffs. High prices!

b. Fast food outlets. Hamburgers, tacos, and other sandwiches purchased through a window while standing in a line of customers. Low prices.

c. Coffee shops. A limited menu; seating and parking for 25–50 customers; breakfast, lunch, and dinner available. Low to moderate prices.

d. Steak houses. Salad bar, broiled steaks, informal attire, liquor service, casual atmosphere; young people or students serve as waiters, cocktail waitresses, and oversee the steaks as they are barbequed. Moderate to high prices.

If you are considering the restaurant industry as a career area, you will want to analyze each of these company types to determine their competitive position within the industry. Which will be most responsive to industry trends? Which will be in the best position to capitalize upon the newest trends?

Another important reason for gaining understanding is that company-types influence earning potential. While two different companies may offer a similar job, the earning potential can be radically different. Here's another illustration to show why you'll want to do your shopping:

ABC Industrial Controls Company hires people to sell its products. One of their sales persons has been given a territory and a sales quota for the year. If the sales quota is reached, a compensation package (salary + commission + bonus) which will amount to $13,000 will be offered. If the quota is surpassed, additional earnings will be paid because of the commission arrangement.

The employer has designed each aspect of the compensation package with a purpose. The base salary offers the worker a sense of security. The bonus is offered if the quota is achieved; this gives the sales person a realizeable goal which helps to motivate. The commission is offered to further stimulate and motivate, to sell more than the quota.

But if the quota is surpassed, doubled, or tripled, the employer will change things next year. You see, next year, the employer will either reduce the physical size of the sales territory or raise the sales quota or both! Why? Because the employer has determined that the sales people should be paid between $12,000 and $20,000 for their work; as they grow in experience and seniority, they should progress along the scale from 12 to 20. If they earn more, the conclusion is that they must not be sufficiently challenged. Another concern, morale problems will quickly arise among the sales staff when one or two are receiving disproportionately higher earnings.

However, the employees were not given this insight into company practices when they were hired. They were told about salary, bonus, and commission in a manner which seemed that earning potential was unlimited. No information was offered about the 12–20 scale and the experience/seniority requirement. Employees didn't know that they should ask.

Sales persons can work in more lucrative environments. A major contrast is seen in the XYZ investment brokerage firm, which also needs people to sell its products. Here, each sales person is called a broker; investment vehicles such as stocks, bonds, warrants, puts, and calls are sold to clients. No set geographic territory is established, a minimal quota is designated, and increasingly lucrative rewards are offered as sales grow higher and higher. After the initial two or three years, the employee will probably be earning $30,000; however, this figure could be $100,000. After a few more years (8–10), the broker will probably earn $50,000; however, he could also be earning $400,000.

Is this fair? Why did one person earn such an immense salary while a counterpart in the other company and industry faced a much more modest earnings future?

Fair or not, it's reality! This is one of the reasons for your need to take charge of your future. Knowing about the alternatives will prevent you from selling industrial controls when you could have been spending the same 40 to 60 hours each week selling investment services. Selecting a field upon which to build your career from within our sophisticated environment will be easily accomplished when you have sufficient knowledge of the industry alternatives. Only after becoming aware of the many, many alternatives and options will you be ready to initiate a career selection process!

Use the following outline to identify and better understand the company-types in the industry you have selected.

1. *Organizational structures.* Ask about the types of organizations currently competing in the industry. You will want to know which structure will be most efficient and the reasons behind that fact. Determine the "key" jobs under each organizational structure.

    a. What different organizational structures are being used? When and under what circumstances does each structure work most efficiently.

    b. Do the companies use centralized or decentralized management techniques? How does this influence opportunities for advancement?

    c. How many departments exist within the companies? What are the approximate number of employees in each department?

    d. What is the key functional department? Which department does most of the top management represent?

2. *Size.* Smaller firms can be more responsive to changes in the market; larger firms get special advantages because of their ability to deal in large quantities. Determine the advantages and disadvantages associated with the size of each company type.

a. What is the yearly sales volume?
b. How many customers are served each year? What is the diversity of customers? Are most of the sales made to one or two major customers?
c. How many product lines exist within each company-type?

3. Human resources. Identify the opportunities for people of your qualifications by looking at the makeup of the current management team. Compare the company-types and their techniques of developing managers.

a. What is the percentage of total manpower allotted to each functional department?
b. What is the ratio of blue collar to white collar workers?
c. What is the educational and experience background of department heads and corporate officers?
d. What are the age ranges of management personnel? Are young people offered the opportunity for management?

4. Relationship with industry trends. Evaluate the relationship between each company-type and the industry trends.

a. How do company activities match with present industry trends?
b. Are the companies preparing themselves for future changes within the industry?
c. What techniques are being used to stay attuned to industry trends?

5. Range of goods and services. Judge each company-type's ability to grow larger and more profitable by looking at the range of goods and services being offered. Look for a type which can effectively penetrate many markets; potential for both growth and stability is more assured. A company which has limited personnel or product lines and continues to concentrate upon one or two major markets may be in a high-risk situation.

a. What range of goods and services are being offered by company-types within the industry?
b. Does the potential exist for expansion of goods and services?
c. Does potential exist for capturing an increased portion of the current market segment with the present line of goods and services?

6. Growth projections. Compare and contrast each company-type's plans for growth. Look for a plan which best fits a person with your skills and which coincides with industry trends.

a. What are the projections for sales growth?
b. What new products and services are being considered?
c. Are new geographic locations being considered?
d. Are mergers or acquisitions planned?

III. Evaluating a Prospective Employer

Now that you are aware of the industry and the competition, look at a specific company.

Information about public companies is readily available by asking the research department of investment organizations and consulting the references in Appendix B. Check with the investment organizations in your area to compile a complete list of companies being researched; copies of their research reports are available to you at no cost.

Information about private companies is best required by speaking with the companies themselves. Call them! Represent yourself as an individual who is reviewing their career plan. Ask for information and advice about the field and its career potential for a person like yourself. This approach will work. Consider this, you have just flattered the individual by asking for an opinion. When was the last time you said no when someone asked you for advice? And it will be today's information, right from someone who is involved. What questions should you ask?

The factors and considerations to be used in evaluating a prospective employer include: company organization and description, relationship of the company's future plans to industry and economic trends, financial position, job function, management development assistance, compensation, location, training, and people.

The following sections will offer some ideas in data gathering and evaluation.

1. Company organization and description. In this section, determine the company's major strengths and weaknesses. You will be looking for a company whose major activity coincides with your field of interest. Look for a company whose managers have a background similar to the one you are building for yourself.

The following questions will guide you in researching the company's organization and description:

a. Is the company large, medium, or small in relation to the other companies in the industry? Does its size pose any limitations?
b. What is the number of employees?
c. How long has the company been in operation compared with other companies operating within the same industry?
d. What are the company's sources of revenue? What is the major source of revenue?

e. What has been the rate of company growth in size and profits over the past five years?

f. Do the company's plans for the future coincide with industry trends and with the trends within our economy?

g. How do their employees, competitors, creditors, and customers regard the company's reputation and personality?

h. Is the professional ability of the company leaders well respected by their peers and competitors? Does their management expertise equip the company with a good opportunity for success? What past experience is held by each member of the management team?

i. Are there any major personal battles raging within the management structure?

j. Do legal or labor problems of major consequence exist?

2. *Company's plans for the future.* Look at the relationship between the company's plans for the future and industry trends within our country's economy. Excellent sources for industry and economy research data are banks, investment research and brokerage organizations, and government agencies.

The following questions will help:

a. Is the company equipped to compete within the industry in the future? Does the company have the necessary resources to meet the needs of its customers in the future?

b. Have future plans for diversification or redirecting product lines been made?

c. Does the company have the necessary management talent to compete within the industry in the future?

d. Will current legislative actions have an effect upon company growth and profits?

e. What are the forecasts for the industry and economy within the company's geographic area of business?

3. *Financial position.* Study the financial statements of the company to determine the major source of revenue. Assess the company's potential for future success by comparing this information with that obtained in the previous section.

Libraries offer many financial reports and literature to acquaint you with a company's financial position. Some of the most valuable references are: *Thomas' Register of American Manufacturers; Standard & Poor's Corporation Records; Poor's Register of Directors and Executives; Dun & Bradstreet Reference Book,* and company annual reports.

Questions to be raised are:

a. What percentage is the major source of revenue contributing to total revenues? Is it planned to continue to comprise the same percentage of total revenues?

b. Is the company highly leveraged? What will be the consequences of an abrupt change in the market?

c. Are profits being reinvested into the company or are they being filtered out by management and owners?

d. What expense factors are categorized as fixed and variable costs? Is an abrupt change in fixed or variable costs profits detected from year to year?

4. *Job function.* Understand the employer's intent and purpose in designing the job and his perceptions of the job function so that you will know what he will be expecting. Understanding the job clearly is also needed for you to determine its potential for helping you achieve your career objectives.

Ask these questions:

a. Have your formal education and personal background prepared you sufficiently for this job?

b. Will you be utilizing your strongest assets in performing the job function thus providing you with the greatest opportunity for success?

c. Is the skill developed in performing this job applicable to other companies and industries?

d. What will be the required time in travel and time away from home? Will you be required to work late hours, weekends, or holidays?

e. Will you be performing a variety of assignments as opposed to a long range single assignment?

f. What future opportunities exist within the company after achieving a high level of competence within this job function?

g. What additional formal education or training will be necessary?

5. *Management development assistance.* You will want to know about the assistance offered by the company to qualify their employees for more responsible positions.

a. Does a management development program exist within the company? Who is eligible for participation on the program?

b. Are formal training or continued education subsidies offered to assist in personal development?

c. What techniques are used to evaluate your work performance?

d. What experience is required to earn promotions? Are promotions based upon tenure or performance or both?

e. Will changes in location, working hours and conditions, and benefits accompany promotions?

f. Does the company consider only its current employees for promotion when an opening occurs? Are "outsiders" hired regularly for openings in top slots within the company?

6. Compensation. Determine the average starting salary for the position and the long-range salary potential. Also, understand the frequency and basis for salary reviews.

An important concept is to consider the whole compensation package instead of salary alone. Review the two job offers in Figure 3–2. Which compensation package is more attractive?

Figure 3–2

	Job A*	Job B†
Salary............................	$15,000	$12,600
Use of automobile....................	—	1,620
Insurance (health, life, dental).........	40	350
Profit sharing or bonus...............	—	850
Total.......................	$15,040	$15,420

* Job A offers stock options to employees after five years tenure; salary reviews are conducted yearly.

† Job B conducts salary reviews every six months; 100 percent tuition reimbursement is offered to employees.

The salary in Job A differs from that in Job B by $2,400; however, the total compensation package in Job B is greater in total dollar value. This amount may be even higher if you are planning to attend school in the evenings or if you earn a larger bonus or if your family happens to need extensive medical attention which would be covered by the insurance. Another important factor is the merit salary review every six months which offers the conscientious worker an opportunity to realize rapid salary growth.

The compensation package in Job B is greater than that in Job A; however, the amount may not necessarily be greater for everyone. For example, an individual may not want insurance coverage and desires to drive his own special automobile. For him, Job A may still have a greater usable compensation package. Evaluate each opportunity in relation to its ability to satisfy your needs.

7. Location. Consider the many ramifications of having to relocate you and your family: community services (e.g. safety, police, health, welfare, utilities, school system, and city government), opportunities for continued education, proximity to desirable housing and recreational facilities, availability of housing, exposure to other professionals within your field of interest, climate and its influence upon your family's health, cost of having to at least maintain your present standard of living (see Figure 3–3), and the availability of transportation facilities including highways, airports, bus terminals, and train stations.

Location will be of greater importance to some. Separation from family and friends may cause emotional stress; a financial burden may loom

Figure 3–3

Computing salary equivalents*

Northeast		South	
Boston, Mass.	119	Atlanta, Ga.	91
Buffalo, N.Y.	105	Baltimore, Md.	100
Hartford, Conn.	104	Dallas, Texas	90
New York, N.Y.	116	Houston, Texas	92
Philadelphia, Pa.	104	Washington, D.C.	108
North Central		**West**	
Chicago, Ill.	101	Denver, Colo.	100
Cincinnati, Ohio	99	Los Angeles, Calif.	95
Cleveland, Ohio	102	San Diego, Calif.	95
Detroit, Mich.	103	San Francisco, Calif.	104
Milwaukee, Wis.	103	Seattle, Wash.	100
Minneapolis, Minn.	104	Honolulu, Hi.	124

Source: Comparative Cost Index, Bureau of Labor Statistics, U.S. average (cities) 100.

Example 1. If you are offered $22,000 from a Los Angeles employer, what is the equivalent salary in New York considering the variance in cost of living?

$$\frac{\text{N.Y. index}}{\text{L.A. index}} \times \text{L.A. salary} = \text{N.Y. salary}$$

$$\frac{116}{95} \times \$22,000 = \$26,862$$

Example 2. What is the San Francisco equivalent of a $12,000 offer in Cincinnati?

$$\frac{\text{S.F. index}}{\text{Cin. index}} \times \text{Cincinnati salary} = \text{San Francisco salary}$$

$$\frac{104}{99} \times \$12,000 = \$12,606$$

* Use the index in the examples to compute equivalent salary offers in different states.

when long distance telephone calls and travel costs incurred through visits are tabulated. A recent graduate refused an attractive offer from a corporation in Michigan because the cost for round trip air fare from Michigan to Las Vegas was so high. Gambling was his favorite hobby!

Location will be of great importance when beginning a career where your business will be based upon repeat service to clients. Examples of such industries are: life insurance sales, a law practice, or management consulting. Insure that the location will afford a sufficient field of prospective clients. Consider also, that after establishing such a business, relocating to another state or part of the country will necessitate "starting all over again" in building a new clientele.

Therefore, recognize the limitations involved in selecting the location when evaluating your future employer.

8. Training. If you are new or have limited experience in the industry of your choice, consider joining a company who offers a training program.

A few years of training and experience with an industry leader will place you in a very good bargaining position; you may elect to stay with the company or look for other opportunities outside the firm. If you decide to change employers after you have been trained by the leaders in the industry, you will look very attractive to any of their large competitors and to smaller firms who plan to grow into the same field. This approach offers a low-risk, high-dividend alternative to the tenuous sink or swim proposition offered by some of the smaller firms who are unable to provide training.

Training programs are designed to:

a. Inform the new employee about the company makeup and overall operation.
b. Supplement college studies with company techniques and processes.
c. Be an opportunity for employer and employee to view each other in preparation for the relationship ahead.

Content and technique of training vary widely. No one type of program is better than another; each is tailored to satisfy the employer's need and policy. Some programs are designed to meet the specific needs of the employee.

Evaluating the quality of the training is a necessary prerequisite before deciding upon the employer. Who will be doing the training? Are they highly respected, proven leaders in their fields of expertise? While approaches toward new employee preparation and training programs may differ widely, you will want to determine your chances of being trained "by the best" and that your training will equip you with skills which will be applicable in other departments or companies.

Guard against being too specialized or trained to perform a function which is peculiar to only one company.

9. *People.* Here we come to one of the most important considerations in the employer evaluation process: Do you *like* your prospective supervisor and co-workers? Be sure. The importance of being able to communicate effectively with your prospective employer and co-workers, to interrelate with them easily, to respect them as people, and to enjoy being with them cannot be overemphasized. Having an enjoyable interpersonal relationship will increase your chances of success.

Many highly promising individuals have experienced frustrations and failures because they were unable to work efficiently because of personal conflicts within the company.

While negative factors often inhibit employee performance, the lack of positive factors also cause problems such as a lack of motivation which prevents an employee from realizing full potential.

Summary

Go shopping! Get started by reviewing your current employer and industry or growth industries in your portion of the country.

Conduct industry analysis by gathering information about the following:
    a. *Influence of population, economy, legislation, and technology upon the industry.*
    b. *Industry background.*
    c. *Present general trends.*
    d. *Problems of the industry.*
    e. *Government's impact upon the industry.*
    f. *Future trends.*

Conduct company-type analysis by reviewing the following:
    a. *Organizational structures.*
    b. *Size.*
    c. *Manpower.*
    d. *Relationship with industry trends.*
    e. *Range of goods and services.*
    f. *Growth projections.*

Evaluate a prospective employer by considering the following:
    a. *Company organization.*
    b. *Plans for the future.*
    c. *Financial position.*
    d. *Job function.*
    e. *Management development assistance.*
    f. *Compensation.*
    g. *Location.*
    h. *Training.*
    i. *People.*

4 | *Interview yourself first*

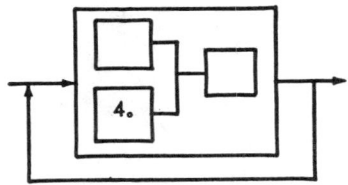

The Ability to Make Effective Career Decisions is Based upon a Thorough Understanding of Your Personal Resources

A career or profession which is closely aligned with your strongest skills, satisfying to your needs, and in consonance with your values will offer you the highest chance for success and happiness.

What are your personal resources? Upon which resources will you base your career? You will enjoy finding the answers to these questions:

1. Background

Which aspects of your background represent your most *impressive achievements?*

The following questions are posed to identify your skills and abilities. But, also, as you state the most impressive achievements, determine why you felt so. Your answers will offer a better idea of what is important to you. Your values will be becoming more apparent.

If you feel that you have no impressive achievements in some of the categories, that fact tells us plenty. It may reveal that your abilities in the area are not your strongest and that your values may not be aligned in that area either.

Look at the method you have used to measure your achievements, i.e., dollars earned, recognition, service to others; the technique you have selected conveys an important message about what is important to you.

Remember, the answers to these questions are for your use only; disregard their relationship to employers and hiring practices. Do not feel limited in your responses; only you will see your answers.

Write a short synopsis of your most impressive achievements **related** to each of the following categories.

a. Work experience:_____

_____

_____

_____

b. College studies:_____

_____

_____

_____

c. Academic records:_____

_____

_____

_____

d. Personal motivation:_____

_____

_____

_____

e. Psychological tests:_____

_____

_____

_____

f. Achievement/aptitude tests:_____

_____

_____

_____

g. Summer and part-time jobs_____

_____

_____

h. Hobbies:_____

_____

_____

_____

i. Honors/distinctions:_____

_____

_____

j. Precollege years: _____

_____

_____

_____

k. Verbal/written communication skills:_____

_____

_____

_____

l. Other activities:_____

_____

_____

_____

2. Results of Work Experience

What benefits did your previous employers receive as a result of your work?

View yourself as an employer views prospective employees. The questions listed in this section represent the areas of great concern by employers. Employees are reviewed in light of their ability to contribute to the company goals.

You will want to know the answers to these questions to assist in identifying where you will fit and what your major contribution could be.

Answer the following questions by giving the following information:

Describe exactly what you did.

Present information about the circumstances.

Identify the results for which you were solely responsible and as part of a team.

Determine the benefits to the company, to other employees, and to you.

a. Were your efforts instrumental in company cost reduction?

_____

_____

_____

_____

b. Did you stimulate additional sales or identify new markets?

_____

_____

_____

_____

c. Were you responsible for enlarging the current line of products or services?

_____

_____

_____

_____

d. Were you responsible for improvements by redefining job functions within the company?

_____

_____

_____

_____

e. Did you improve company operations by installing new systems or procedures?

_____

_____

_____

_____

f. What circumstances surrounded your promotions?

_____

_____

_____

_____

g. What contributions have you made to your department, to its operation, to the employee morale?

_____

_____

_____

_____

h. Were you responsible for identifying new company policies, directions, or objectives?

_____

_____

_____

_____

i. Were you awarded recognition or honors for works within your industry?

_____

_____

_____

_____

3. Personal Preferences in Work Situations

Consider the following statements in relation to your preferences in work situations *most of the time*. Place an X in the appropriate column.

Yes   No

____ ____ Able to reprimand employees.

____ ____ Need being offered praise when I do a good job.

Yes   No

——— ——— Careful with details.

——— ——— Constant contact with people is important.

——— ——— Desire leadership responsibilities and power.

——— ——— Dislike complicated procedures.

——— ——— Dislike making decisions.

——— ——— Dislike problems unless there are standard ways to solve them.

——— ——— Dislike repetitious tasks.

——— ——— Dislike telephone interruptions.

——— ——— Dislike telling people unpleasant things.

——— ——— Don't mind working on one project for a long time uninterruptedly.

——— ——— Don't usually get inspired.

——— ——— Efficiency may be impaired by interpersonal unrest.

——— ——— Employer must respect my high quality work.

——— ——— Enjoy having several projects going on at the same time.

——— ——— Enjoy learning a new skill more than using it.

——— ——— Enjoy little or no supervision.

——— ——— Enjoy using skills already acquired.

——— ——— Need to feel my job is important.

——— ——— Follow inspirations or emotions.

——— ——— Good physical working conditions are highly important.

——— ——— Having an efficient supervisor is crucial.

——— ——— Impatient when there are too many complicated details to remember.

——— ——— Interested in concepts rather than tasks.

——— ——— Interested in prestige, status, and recognition.

——— ——— Large amount of freedom on the job is necessary.

——— ——— Like quiet for concentration.

——— ——— Like solving new problems.

——— ——— Like to adapt to changing situations.

——— ——— Like to plan the work and be able to get it finished on schedule.

——— ——— Like to please people or help them.

——— ——— Like to serve and work with humanity.

——— ——— Like to think before acting.

——— ——— Like variety and some distraction.

——— ——— Make decisions impersonally, sometimes ignoring people's wishes.

——— ——— May not like to interrupt one project for a more urgent one.

——— ——— May start too many projects and lose control.

——— ——— Not very interested in people's feelings. Low personal sensitivity.

Yes   No

—— —— Opportunity for very rapid career growth is important.

—— —— Patient with complicated situations.

—— —— Patient with routine details.

—— —— Plenty of autonomy and personal independence is mandatory.

—— —— Procrastinate often.

—— —— Responsibility for people management problems is thrilling.

—— —— Seek out original and creative assignments.

—— —— Steady employment is required.

—— —— Usually act impulsively.

—— —— Very aware of other people and their feelings.

—— —— Want a fast-paced environment.

—— —— Work in bursts of enthusiasm.

—— —— Work on projects which serve society.

4. Temperament Personality Traits

Which words would best describe your personality traits?

Circle the words in the following list which apply to you *most of the time.*

abrupt, absent-minded, active, adaptable, aggressive, ambitious, analytical, arrogant, artistic, avoid responsibility, broad-minded, calm, cautious, cheerful, clumsy, colorful, competitive, complacent, conceited, congenial, conscientious, considerate, consistent, conventional, cooperative, creative, cynical, daring, deceitful, decisive, dependable, detailed, disciplined, drive myself hard, easily annoyed, easily depressed, easily discouraged, easily distracted, easygoing, economical, efficient, egotistical, eloquent, emotional, energetic, enjoy hard work, enthusiastic, even-tempered, exacting, excitable, extroverted, fastidious, forceful, forgetful, fragile, friendly, generally liked by others, generous, good listener, good natured, honest, idealist, imaginative, impatient, impulsive, inconsistent, indecisive, independent, indifferent, informal, individualistic, inhibited, introverted, lack initiative, lazy, leader, lethargic, like to lead, like responsibility, limited interests, logical, loyal, mature, methodical, moody, narrow-minded, nervous, objective, obstinate, often feel lonely, original, outspoken, oversensitive, patient, perfectionist, persuasive, quick, quick-tempered, quiet, realistic, reliable, reserved, resourceful, respectful, restless, retiring, secretive, self-centered, self-confident, self-conscious, self-reliant, sense of humor, shallow, shy, sincere, sociable, systematic, tactful, teamworker, temperamental, thoughtful, timid, tolerant, two-faced, uncertain, unemotional, unreliable, versatile.

58

5. Temperament/Personality Traits Comparison

How do you compare with *most people you know?* The middle point in each scale represents most people you know. Place an "X" on the appropriate spot in each scale which represents you.

Scale Range											
				Most people							
Adaptable	o	o	o	o	o	o	o	o	o	o	Rigid
Aggressive	o	o	o	o	o	o	o	o	o	o	Quiet
Critical	o	o	o	o	o	o	o	o	o	o	Trusting
Diffident	o	o	o	o	o	o	o	o	o	o	Confident
Easily upset	o	o	o	o	o	o	o	o	o	o	Emotionally stable
Extrovert	o	o	o	o	o	o	o	o	o	o	Introvert
Follower	o	o	o	o	o	o	o	o	o	o	Leader
Impulsive	o	o	o	o	o	o	o	o	o	o	Restrained
Modest	o	o	o	o	o	o	o	o	o	o	Brash
Naive	o	o	o	o	o	o	o	o	o	o	Sophisticated
Oversensitive	o	o	o	o	o	o	o	o	o	o	Objective
Resistant	o	o	o	o	o	o	o	o	o	o	Agreeable
Slow	o	o	o	o	o	o	o	o	o	o	Energetic
Slow to anger	o	o	o	o	o	o	o	o	o	o	Quick to anger
Solitary	o	o	o	o	o	o	o	o	o	o	Sociable
Superficial	o	o	o	o	o	o	o	o	o	o	Reflective
Timid	o	o	o	o	o	o	o	o	o	o	Self-assured

6. Abilities Gained Through Formal Education

What can I *do* as a result of each of the courses taken in my field of study?

Construct a grid to assist in taking an inventory of your educational experience. The example below could be used by a person who has studied business administration. Build a grid for *your* field of study.

Answer the following questions for each empty box in the grid:

1. What was studied in this area?
2. What skills have you developed as a result of this study?

List of courses taken in business administration	Field of study: Business administration				
	Accounting	*Management*	*Marketing*	*Finance*	*QBA*
Business communication					
Marketing theory					
Behavior analysis					
Quantitative business analysis					
Principles of finance					
Investment analysis					
Consumer marketing communication					
Advertising					
Portfolio management					
Accounting for management and control					
Taxation					
Cost analysis					

Construct a grid for your field of study; use the space below.

	Field of study:
List of courses taken in	

Ranking of abilities gained through formal education

Review the entries you have made in the previous exercise; rank your abilities according to proficiency achieved. Attempt to substantiate your ranking by referring to grades, professor's remarks, honors achieved, or other impartial sources.

Abilities gained with high proficiency	Facts to substantiate ranking
1.	
2.	
3.	
4.	
5.	
6.	
7.	
8.	
9.	
10.	

7. Abilities Gained Through Work Experience

What can I *do* as a result of the work experience I've gained?

Construct a grid to assist in taking an inventory of your work experience. The example below was used by a person who has experience in four different companies with four separate job functions.

Answer the following questions for each empty box in the grid:

1. What were your responsibilities?
2. What did you do to carry out these responsibilities?
3. What were the results of your efforts?
4. What skills did you develop as a result of this experience?

		Company-time description			
Function		*ABC Company general manager*	*XYZ Company marketing management*	*MNO Company industrial relations*	*RST Company purchasing materials*

General management
  Profit and loss
  Planning
  Organization development
  Finance/control
  Resource utilization
  Policy/procedures					

Industrial relations
  Recruiting/placement
  Wage/salary
  Labor relations
  Management development/
    training
  Safety/security
  Policy/procedures					

Purchasing/material/production
  Manufacturing
  Contracts/agreements/
    buying
  Inventory/control/stores
  Scheduling
  Traffic/shipping/receiving
  Policy/procedures					

Sales/marketing/engineering
  Planning/forecasting
  Services/administration
  Contracts/agreements
  Negotiations
  Customer Relations
  Policy/procedures
  Design
  Product development					

Complete your grid below.

	Company-time description
Function	

Review the entries made in the previous exercise, rank your abilities according to proficiency achieved and substantiate the ranking.

Abilities gained with high proficiency	Facts to substantiate ranking
1.	
2.	
3.	
4.	
5.	
6.	
7.	
8.	
9.	
10.	

8. Values Sought in Work or Occupations[1]

Which of these values do you seek in your work or occupation?

The first step in recognizing your values is to understand the definition of a value. Values represent a belief and a judgment; that which you believe to be true and have judged to be desirable is an expressed value.

Some people place a high premium on material things, friendships

---

[1] G. W. Allport, P. E. Vernon, and L. G. Lindzey, *Study of Values* (Boston: Houghton Mifflin, 1951).

with other people, intellectual ability, social position, or any number of other categories.

Others attempt value identification by expressing passive assent and reiteration of religious commandments, admonitions, and proscriptions. Others adopt the values of people they admire; or rather, they adopt the interests without really understanding the values. This approach offers little or no real sense of satisfaction; sensual, short-lived stimulation is substituted.

Look through the list; read each definition. Write your impression of each value category and its application to you in the space provided for your remark; is it of great importance, of somewhat importance, or of no concern to you?

1. *Altruism*—Regard for/or devotion to the interest of others.

   Remark:_____

2. *Aesthetics*—Dealing with the beautiful; pertaining to the relegation of standards (values) in relation to what is beautiful.

   Remark:_____

3. *Creativity*—Ability to create.

   Remark:_____

4. *Intellectual stimulation*—That which excites one to engage in activity requiring the creative use of the intellect.

   Remark:_____

5. *Independence*—The quality or state of being independent; freedom; self-governing.

   Remark:_____

6. *Achievement*—The act of attaining a desired end, bringing to a successful conclusion; to work conscientiously to achieve goals and to excell.

   Remark:_____

7. *Prestige*—Standing or estimation in the eyes of people; commanding position in men's minds; to attain an admired position.

   Remark:_____

8. *Management*—The act of carrying on and directing business affairs; capacity for managing; executive skill.

   Remark:_____

9. *Economic returns*—Relating to/or based on the production, distribution, and consumption of goods and services; in this case, more particularly, relating to remunerative incentive.

   Remark:_____

10. *Security*—The quality or state of being assured in expectation; free from doubt.

    Remark:_____

11. *Surroundings*—The circumstances, conditions, or objects which form one's environment; work area and its location and appearance.

    Remark:_____

12. *Supervisory relations*—The type and extent of authoritative direction.

    Remark:_____

13. *Associates*—Fellow workers; colleagues.

    Remark:_____

14. *Variety*—The quality or state of having different kinds; specifically different kinds of functions or aspects within one's position.

    Remark:_____

15. *Way of life*—The state of being or acting on a specified scale; a recognizable tendency or quality; regular, continued course or mode.
    Remark:_____

9. Needs Satisfied by Work or Occupation[2]

Which of the following are your needs to be satisfied by work or occupation?

Pick a time when you are in good humor; insure that you are not in a state of depression or under heavy pressures because these conditions will inhibit your objectivity and performance in enumerating and analyzing your needs. Consider this analysis to be an adventure not a chore.

Look through the list; read each definition. Write your impression of each category and its relation to you in the space provided for your remark.

---

[2] H. A. Murray, *Explorations in Personality* (New York: Oxford University Press, 1958).

Achievement: The act of attaining a desired end, bringing to a successful conclusion; to attain goals; to excell; action oriented.

Remark:_____

Deference: Courteous, respectful regard for another's wishes; to cooperate with a leader; to serve willingly.

Remark:_____

Order: To be precise, neat, tidy; to organize and arrange.

Remark:_____

Exhibition: An act or instance of outward display by visible signs or actions; to attract attention; to amuse or excite others.

Remark:_____

Autonomy: The quality or state of existing or capability of existing independently; to resist coercion; to seek freedom.

Remark:_____

Affiliation: The state of being brought or received into a close connection as a member; to form friendships; to join groups.

Remark:_____

Succorance: The state of seeking relief, aid, or sympathy; to adhere to a parent or protector; to be dependent.

Remark:_____

Dominance: The fact or state of being authoritative, controlling, prevailing, or commanding from a superior position; to lead, influence, or control others; to direct the behavior of a group.

Remark:_____

Abasement: The state of having lost or yielded up dignity or prestige; to surrender and accept punishment; to depricate one's self.

Remark:_____

Nurturance:	To help others; to nourish or protect the helpless; to act as a parent.
	Remark:_____
Endurance:	The ability to withstand hardships, adversity, or stress; perseverance; pursuing tasks to successful completion.
	Remark:_____
Heterosexuality:	Relating to or marked by sexual orientation toward members of the opposite sex.
	Remark:_____
Aggression:	The practice of making attacks or approachments; to ridicule, harm, or belittle a person; to assault.
	Remark:_____

After a break, read your answers for exercises 1–9. Become thoroughly familiar with the picture drawn by your responses for each question. When you feel you know yourself, answer the questions in the next chapter.

Summary

The ability to make effective career decisions is based upon a thorough understanding of your personal resources.

The personal factors relevant to career decision making are your capabilities, values, and needs.

The following areas are to be reviewed in gaining self-awareness:
  a. *Past impressive achievements.*
  b. *Benefits to former employers as a result of your work experience.*
  c. *Personal preferences in work assignments.*
  d. *Temperament personality traits.*
  e. *Comparison of personality traits with others.*
  f. *Identification, ranking, and verification of capabilities gained through education and work experience.*
  g. *Values sought in work or occupation.*
  h. *Needs satisfied by work or occupation.*
Each of the above areas will offer insight into all three areas: capabilities, values, and needs.

5 | *The ten principles of career development*

In chapter 4, you identified your interests, abilities and personality traits. In order to understand how your personal resources relate to the realities of employment practices, you should memorize the ten principles of career development:

1. People who hold positions which directly affect sales and profits are on the freeway to the top.
2. People are paid according to the worth of the position to the company and the person's ability to perform the function of that position.
3. Skills development is the key to job promotions.
4. Your selection of additional education or training opportunities should be based on skill development.
5. Chances for career success are greater when your strongest skills are those required for top performance on the job.
6. All employers look for the same five traits to identify desirable candidates: decision-making skills, communication skills, interpersonal skills, achievement record, career direction.
7. High achievers are in constant demand.
8. A company environment which attracts and retains High Achievers includes:
   a. opportunity for achievement,
   b. recognition for achievement,
   c. opportunity for personal growth,
   d. advancement through the organization,
   e. responsibility and authority for the job to be done.
9. Management practice which enhances career development provides for:
   a. exposure to many supervisors,

b. supervisor-employee openness,
c. continuous feedback,
d. skills growth through team assignments,
e. performance reviews,
f. promotion on merit.
10. Career decisions must be based upon positive factors.

Each of these principles is discussed and some are illustrated with an example of a person facing a career decision.

1. Influence Sales and Profits

People who hold positions which can most directly influence sales and profits are on the freeway to the top in the company. Any other type of job in the company will be a career dead end. Earnings, opportunity for rapid advancement, social status and prestige within the company, responsibility, challenge and adventure, and the opportunity to be creative and original are closely associated with the source-of-profit job concept.

Joseph Stevens

Joe is a personnel specialist in a public accounting firm; he is directly responsible for recruiting experienced managers for the firm. The major source of profit for the firm is conducting financial control audits of publicly held companies. The partners in the firm, the people at the top, are accountants, CPAs. Because of the nature of the firm, Joe is in a career dead end. Regardless of the quality of recruiting skills, the personnel specialist will not be in a position to create profits and will, therefore, be relegated to a limited growth (and limited earnings!) position.

What would happen if Joe were to join an executive search firm? The source of profit for such a firm is recruiting qualified candidates for corporate clients who pay a handsome fee for the service. The executive search firm also employs an accountant, a necessary resource in every firm. But, here, the roles and career potentials are reversed. The personnel specialist is in the growth position while the accountant is in the dead-end job.

2. Know What a Job Is Worth to the Employer

Earnings and salary potential are based upon the worth of a specific position within the company. People are not paid according to their worth but rather according to the worth of the position to the company and the person's ability to perform the functions of that position.

If the president of the world's largest corporation earning $1,000,000 each year in salary were to be hired to wipe windows at a car wash, he would be paid about $3 an hour because that job is only worth $3 an hour.

And if he were poor at wiping windows, he would not be worth that.

A popular question surfaces often, "What type of job will allow me to make the most money the fastest?"

Consider becoming a commissioned salesperson. You will be paid in accordance with your ability to generate profit for the company. The real estate salesperson in your area earns a percentage of every sale. After three or four months of training, many salespersons have made their first sale and earned a commission of several thousand dollars. If you were to list and sell one house each week for $100,000, your earnings for one year might be $150,000 plus! The exciting thought is that you could sell 10 houses each week . . . or none. In this job, earnings are based upon *results,* not time invested or effort or seniority of job title or sex or heritage or education level.

Recall the important principle: *You will be paid in accordance with your ability to generate profit for the company.* Some jobs cannot generate profit because of the nature of the position (e.g., bookkeeper, warehouse manager, personnel administrator).

The real estate sales position was selected as an example because of the large dollar value associated with the product being sold. If we were to take a successful real estate salesperson earning $150,000 each year and place him/her in the position of selling brushes, door-to-door, to the same type of customers (families who buy houses), that salesperson would earn about $12,000 each year because the amount of profit generated for the employer would be considerably lower and so would the salesperson's value to the company. However, if that salesperson were allowed to call upon commercial accounts where each customer might purchase thousands of brushes, the profit generated would be higher and so would the earnings be increased.

3. Develop Your Skills

Skills development is the key to job promotions. An employee who develops and displays the necessary skills required to maintain a higher level of responsibilities will most likely be the person to be promoted.

Your career will develop as far and as rapidly as your skills develop.

Skills development precedes job promotions which make up the concept of career development. Although sometimes career development is measured by reviewing job promotions, be sure to recognize that skills development comes first.

John Skinner

John was hired as a staff analyst into the corporate office of a metals manufacturing firm. Located in San Francisco, John enjoyed a prestigious title, pleasant location, adequate salary, opportunity to work on the staff of one of the vice presidents, and the promise of opportunity for advancement.

After three years of successful performance, the firm asked John to accept a line management position in one of their subsidiaries in Louisiana. John refused. The firm was offering John an outstanding opportunity—line management responsibilities and *training to develop the management skills he would need for further promotions*. Instead, he resigned and accepted a staff analyst position with another firm in the San Francisco area.

John sincerely aspires to a management position, but he will never be able to achieve this goal unless he develops the skills first. Accepting another staff assignment will limit his promotability. In a few years he may be fraught with career frustration and stagnation.

Skills development is also a key concept when considering career mobility. The following questions and accompanying responses will be of interest.

Question: How can I insure career mobility? Some of my friends say they are stuck in one company and cannot move. What do they mean by that and how can I keep it from happening to me?

Response: Your friends may be making the point that they cannot change jobs outside of their current employer's company because the salary for which they could qualify would be considerably lower. To go a step further, the skills they have developed are peculiar to the current employer . . . and are irrelevant to assignments outside that specific firm. For example, a manager of job scheduling for a service firm must have an in-depth understanding of each client's needs, eccentricities, and environment along with a thorough awareness of the firm's staff because it is the manager's job to select the proper combination of staff to service the client each year. That knowledge may require several years of experience to gain; but the precious information is of little value outside the firm.

You can insure career mobility by developing skills which are transferable. If the job requires that you spend a major portion of your time in developing knowledge and skills peculiar to one company, pass up the job.

Question: I am a buyer for Ohrbach's, a substantial retailing firm. I do the women's outerwear (coats). I spent the first three years of my career with May Co., the last two years with Ohrbach's. Well, Ohrbach's is planning to centralize their buying function in New York. I am married and cannot move. What career alternatives shall I consider?

Response: The skills you have developed at Ohrbach's will be the basis for determining your alternatives. Notice I emphasized *skills,* not *experience.* What are your skills? When reviewing the following alternatives, compare your skills to those required in each alternative:

Your firm's competitors which perform the buying function in your area

Transfer from buying (merchandise management) to sales and sales management (store management)

Seek a sales or designer position with one of the manufactur-ers or designers which supply merchandise to your firm

Consider a position with one of the firms which manufacture and market the equipment and services purchased by Ohr-bach's (e.g., display racks, advertising displays, data process-ing equipment for inventory control and cash registers, etc.)

Question: How can I change careers without taking a salary cut?

Response: The secret is to change to a career where your current set of skills is relevant.

The salary range associated with your current job is determined by measuring the worth of the position to the company and the job market for qualified candidates for the position. The salary being paid to you is determined within the range by considering your skill level and tenure with the company.

If you wish to change careers without taking a salary cut, select a position where your current skills are relevant. For example, an administrative manager in a life insurance firm may change careers, move to the jewelry retailing field. The new job is to manage the office consisting of accountant, bookkeeper, inventory clerk, secretary, receptionist, and handyman. All previous administrative experience is relevant. However, if that same person wanted to change to a career such as computer sales, a considerable amount of training and new skills are needed.

4. Select the Right Educational Opportunities

Should you pursue a different college degree? . . . an initial college degree? . . . go to law school? . . . earn a master's degree?

The principle of skills development being the key to job promotions and thus career development is relevant to this question. When faced with which school or academic program to select, ask yourself, "What skills will I be developing if I pursue a different college degree? . . . earn a master's degree? etc."

Select the school by screening the faculty and curriculum. Once you know the objective of your matriculation, you will be in an excellent position to evaluate faculty strengths and curriculums. The school's overall reputation is not as relevant as the school's ability to give you what you want.

Some careers/employers/companies require a specific college or curriculum before entry. The reasons may be technically valid but they may also be vague, such as:

XYZ University's entrance requirements are very high; if we hire someone from that school, we are getting one of the nation's best.

Graduating from college (or MBA school, law school, etc.) requires persistence, attention to detail, intelligence, and drive; we want that kind of person.

Candidates who have graduated with a master's degree are a little more mature and are more likely to have a realistic view about work and careers.

The following three questions relating to education and skills often surface from persons considering a job change:

Question: I am a 34-year-old copywriter for an advertising agency making $850 each month. I would like to be an account executive, but I am told that I do not qualify because of my lack of business experience. Should I use my savings to finance a master's degree in business?

Response: The average salary for new business graduates with a master's degree is over $1,500 each month; in two years, inflation could push that salary to over $1,700. In general, you could double your earning by going back to school for two years. Lost income for two years at your current earnings rate will be about $20,000. Tuition and books could add up to another $10,000. Both the new earning power and the lost income should be considered before making the decision.

Successful account executives are marketing professionals who have excellent sales skills. Marketing planning and strategy can be studied in the classroom; sales skills are developed on the job, in the field. If you are sincere in becoming an account executive, meet with several of them to gain a better understanding of the functional process they perform and the skills required. You may find that a full-time position with a firm which offers sales training supplemented by part-time enrollment in a business school will be the right combination for you.

Question: My college degree and the career I have pursued for the last eight years have earned me the designation "professional." Several of my neighbors are tradespeople who earn more money and have more freedom than I. They are union em-

Response: ployees. Do you think I should give up this seemingly hopeless quest to become a business executive and join a union?

Response: What are your objectives? You mention money and freedom. If they are your primary objectives, evaluate each career alternative on the bases of those criteria.

Joining a union is another matter. The bargaining power an individual gains by joining a union is awe inspiring. An employer may be able to turn a deaf ear to one employee's demands, but the full work force organized through a union can extract any reasonable demand from an employer. However . . .

Union membership cannot give you the things which motivate all successful people, such as: achievement, recognition, the work itself, advancement, personal growth. While the union can assist in salary negotiations, working conditions, company policies and other areas, true job satisfaction can only be gained through the proper match between you and your job assignment. Managers and top executives are not in a union because union membership cannot give them what they want.

Question: I have been told several times that I am "overqualified." Should I conceal information about my work experience or my education when I go job searching? In fact, I have offered to accept a salary cut in some instances just to get into the job. Why am I being passed over?

Response: Turnover, the process of acquiring and then losing an employee, is very costly to an employer. The cost is measured in dollars by affixing value to recruiting and interviewing time, training effort, reduction in department efficiency when revenue-producing employees must slow their productivity to adjust to the new employee, employee's salary, and employee fringe benefits (which cost the employer an additional sum equal to 25 percent of the employee's salary or more).

An employer will not want to hire an applicant for a position unless he or she appears to be a proper match for the assignment in terms of salary, education, and skills. A poor match means rapid turnover. "Overqualified" means poor match—turnover problems. Accepting a lower salary than was earned on a previous job may also lead to job dissatisfaction, short tenure, and turnover.

5. Develop the Skills That the Job Requires

Chances for career success and personal happiness will be maximized when your strongest skills are those required for top performance on the job. You probably view yourself as versatile; you can fit into a variety of job assignments and perform them well. However, you will enjoy the highest levels of achievement in those job assignments which are aligned with your strengths.

The concept is straightforward and logical. A complicater surfaces; it is called the *promotion*.

Daniel Anthony

Dan is a well-respected research engineer working with one of the nation's most promient aircraft manufacturing firms. His hard work, persistence, attention to detail, and understanding of the most recent engineering concepts have helped him to earn a reputation as one of the firm's top engineers.

When Dan joined the firm, he acted as an assistant to one of the senior engineers; his assignments were rather technical in nature but always well-defined for him. As he sharpened his technical and judgmental skills, Dan was assigned more and more of the research on wing-stress configurations. He began to specialize in the wing-stress field, needed less direction and gained greater visibility and exposure within the firm. With his sharpened technical skills and growing reputation, Dan was soon selected for a department manager assignment without consideration of the fact that he had no management skills, training, or experience.

After 18 months, he had decided that he was unqualified for the job, found it unfulfilling, and requested a transfer back to the technical staff. The reasons:

a. Dan's greatest strength was his technical specialist skill.

b. The basis for success as a department manager included skills such as motivating, supervising, conducting performance reviews, budgeting, and program scheduling.

c. Dan had not developed the necessary skills and was unwilling to cope with his low performance level while he developed these skills on the job.

d. His chances for career success as a manager are not maximized because his greatest strengths are in another field.

6. Master the Five Traits That All Employers Look For

My research has indicated that each company designs its own selection model. Although this apparent "reinventing the wheel" occurs in each company and in each department of each company, one cannot prove the process to be inefficient. The reason is that each company has specific needs and utilizes procedures and processes which are peculiar to its operation. Thus, each selection model will include selection criteria designed to identify candidates which fit both the general and the specific needs of the company.

The selection criteria used by more than 100 diverse companies show clearly that a few common criteria are used by each and every employer regardless of industry, company type, or job function. In addition, each employer uses criteria which are peculiar to the specific needs of the company and type of business. Employers use each category of criteria, *common* and *specific,* for a different purpose:

a. Common is used to identify the traits and characteristics of a high achiever; and

b. Specific is used to evaluate the fit between the candidate and the specific needs of the company. As job content differs, so does the range and type of technical skills required. Therefore, the actual assessing of the candidate's technical skills and the matching of these skills to those required to perform the entry-level job falls under the category of *specific selection* criteria.

Focus upon the following list of common criteria; look for relevance between the characteristics of the high achiever and the list. The items on the lists are not ranked to represent priority, nor is one item weighted more heavily than the others for our purpose.

Decision-making style

Every employer is concerned with the candidate's basis for judgment and decision-making style. Candidates who can prove that they make decisions with facts rather than emotion or with guesses are the candidates in demand. "Why did you take your last job? What experience was useful? Why did you select your academic major? What did you get out of the program? How is it relevant to what you want to do now?" Employers use these popular questions to hear about the individual's self-perception, decision-making style, and sense of direction.

For inexperienced candidates, grades are used to predict technical competence in the skills required on the job. But grades are also used to assess drive, persistence, and energy level, which are critical qualities in a successful individual. If a candidate explains a low grade-point average by pointing out that he/she had the ability to do much better but was busy with other things during college life, a negative impression is made upon the employer. Why should the employer conclude that the individual will perform to maximum potential on the job? High achievers work at full potential more times than not. If the high achiever has the ability to get a higher G.P.A. that potential will be realized.

Work experience is most important among experienced candidates; employers look for much more than the responsibilities of the position held. "Were you promoted? If so, why? Were you ever fired from a job? Why? What did you enjoy most about being employed?" Popular questions such as these are used to tune into the candidate's drive for improvement, sense of responsibility, and perception of the causes for promotions and growth.

Communications skills

The ability to communicate verbally on a one-to-one basis is the critical skill. Possessing an ability in oral expression includes: fluency in expressing thoughts, selecting appropriate language, adequacy of vocabulary, correct usage of words, clarity and structure of the presentation. However, a great difference exists between oral expression and communication. Communicating does not mean talking. You can talk to a wall, but you cannot communicate with it. Communication is a two-way exchange of information accompanied by mutual understanding. Each person is being sensitive to the other. Verbal communication skills are judged primarily in the job interview.

The next most important communications skill is writing ability for correspondence and reports. After that, speaking skills for presentations before groups are ranked. Neither of these last two kinds of skills is tested before employment unless the major responsibility of the job is to write or to give speeches.

Interpersonal skills

Poise, display of tact, adjustment to others, and generic sociability are desirable traits, but employers are seeking much more than these passive social skills. Employers seek candidates with the proven ability to perform active work harmoniously with groups of people, to be a productive team worker. Successful background experience in relating to peers, handling subordinates, and reporting to superiors is present in the most desirable candidates.

Work experience, club affiliation, extracurricular activities, and hobbies are reviewed to identify a pattern of successful group interface.

Frequently, employers seek candidates with leadership skills. In this context, leadership is defined as the ability to influence the thinking of others. A popular approach to measuring this ability is to review the number and magnitude of elected offices held by the candidates. Appointed offices do not count. Having been elected by a peer group is an impressive indication of the ability to influence the thinking of others.

Achievement record

Drive, energy, physical vitality, and perseverance are indicators of a high achiever. Each candidate's personal background is reviewed to identify these traits, which are embodied in an individual's record of repeated successes, directed energies, and sense of responsibility toward each task.

Responsibility, dependability, reliability, and achievement are popular traits which are used interchangeably by employers. Leadership skill is also mentioned in this context, but here it means the willingness to assume responsibility and bring each task to successful completion with a minimum of supervision and direction. Employers measure these traits by reviewing all aspects of the candidate's background, including work experience, experience, education, club affiliation, extracurricular activities, and hobbies.

Sense of career direction

The most desirable candidates have a thorough understanding of the company, the industry in which it competes, and the job in question. They also have an objective view of personal qualifications and apply a sound reasoning approach to career decision making.

The go-getters, the high achievers use primary and secondary research techniques to understand the industry, company, and job. They read periodicals, books, and brochures to establish a sound basis of understanding. Then, they follow up by approaching people who are currently in the job to discuss the aspects of employment not covered in the printed matter. If they are not acquainted with people in the profession, they make an effort, usually a successful effort, to meet several individuals who can offer the necessary information.

Employers judge the candidate's sense of career direction by asking about the current job objective, the longer-range career objective, and the data used in arriving at these decisions. When the career objective is based upon shallow generalizations and personal assumptions, no matter how specifically the job objective is stated, the employer will not be impressed.

Candidates who point out no sense of career direction are passed over.

These common selection criteria are used by employers to identify the most desirable candidates.

7. Be a High Achiever

High achievers are in constant demand. The term "high achiever" is being used to designate those people who have a high *need* for achievement and, as a result, are more likely to work harder and longer at their job in order to *achieve*. The term does not refer to only those people with high IQs or presidents of countries or athletes with world records.

Men and women imbued with achievement as the motive in their career are exciting to know and desirable to employ. They have four common characteristics. Understanding the characteristics will aid in identifying them and the work environment in which they will thrive.

a. Their time is consistently devoted to thinking about problems, solutions, and better ways of doing things. David C. McClelland, author of *The Achieving Society,* has presented considerable insight into understanding the person who has a high need for achievement. Whether it be termed the "desire for achievement" or the "entrepreneurial spirit," it is that quality in individuals who are consistently concerned with doing things better. Thinking, analyzing, and evaluating alternatives to existing products, processes, or systems consume their free time and idle moments.

b. They desire to assume personal responsibility for assignments or work situations in which problem solving is the task. They seek out and pursue the opportunity to be held responsible for projects so that they will receive a personal sense of achievement satisfaction when the project is completed successfully. Self-confidence is necessarily concomitant with such an individual.

c. High achievers establish realizable goals and are stimulated by moderate risk taking. Selecting achievable goals is easily understandable; these individuals receive their satisfaction from regularly achieving their goals. Setting goals for which the chances of attaining success are remote means that satisfaction seldom can be gained. However, an extremely simple problem in which there is little or no chance of failing offers no real satisfaction in achieving the solution.

d. High achievers want concrete, measurable feedback in order to judge their performance. With this feedback, the individual receives the satisfaction desired. If a job or career does not offer regular feedback in measurable, specific terms, a person with a high need for achievement will not thrive. Positions such as social work, counseling, and teaching do not offer feedback in concrete terms, and therefore high achievers most likely will leave or, if they stay, will be frustrated and dissatisfied.

8. Identify the Companies that Encourage High Achievers

When a position is structured in such a way that it will satisfy the needs of the employee, he/she will be motivated to work and will stay on the job to the mutual benefit of the employee and employer.

Motivation is an internal factor which directs a person's behavior. Motivated behavior is identified and characterized by the following:

a. It is directed toward the achievement of a specific goal.

b. The goal results from *unsatisfied needs.*

c. Motivation will continue until the goal is achieved and the need is satisfied.

What motivates an employee? What makes an employee *want* to do a job? To assume more responsibility? To strive for improvements? To grow?

According to copious research conducted by such behavioral scientists such as Abraham Maslow, Henry A. Murray, Douglas McGregor, Victor H. Vroom, and Frederick Herzberg, truly motivated individuals come by their motivation from within because they are acting to satisfy personal needs. Job satisfaction is received when the inherent human needs are satisfied, but the existence of those needs is the motivator to act.

Addressing the question, "What needs?" requires reflection upon the needs of the high achiever. The need for achievement develops and is exhibited over a long period of time; it is not instantly acquired. People who are highly motivated to achieve have a long history of aspiring to reach high goals, of achieving success in the activities they have pursued, and the intelligence and personal characteristics necessary to achieve. Maslow's hierarchy of needs views motivation as a ranked series of needs. The higher needs are not apparent (or not given attention if apparent) until the lower ranked needs are satisfied. Toward the upper end of the ranking (after physiological needs, safety needs, social needs) are ego needs.

Needs for achievement, competence, independence, self-confidence, knowledge, recognition for achievement, and status are examples of ego needs.

High achievers have activated ego needs; their lower needs are not as prominent.

Here are the five most prominent needs the high achiever has and the ways a company creates an environment which will attract and retain high achievers:

a. Achievement. Establish a clear definition of the job objective and the basis for performance measurement. Gaining a sense of achievement will occur most rapidly and frequently when definite but reachable goals are established. Concrete feedback is necessary. Work results are measured with hard facts such as profits earned, time saved, quantity processed, sales made, etc.

b. Recognition for achievement. Recognition is awarded to those who perform. A true and most satisfying method of offering recognition for work performance is insuring that the individual be held in higher esteem in the eyes of respected peers, supervisors, friends, self, and associates. Sincere expressions of congratulations from co-workers and management are the one most reliable technique of raising esteem. A word expressing admiration, treating the worker to a lunch, or giving a series of unsolicited compliments are irreplaceable recognitions.

Raising the level of an individual's esteem is helped along by offering public acknowledgment of achievement and the presentation of awards in front of assemblies composed of co-workers and top management.

c. Responsibility. Direct responsibility and the necessary authority to do the job are assigned. The employee feels a sense of personal responsibility for the outcome of the assignment; and thus when the assignment is successfully completed, the employee receives a sense of need satisfaction and, therefore, job satisfaction. Assignment of the responsibility is formal and complete; job satisfaction will occur in proportion to the degree of responsibility held and the successful performance of the task.

d. Growth. Assignments are designed which require continued personal or professional growth. Growth is measured in terms of skills development (high achievers seek out areas of activity where new abilities will be developed). Feelings of power and self-esteem are enlarged when abilities become more numerous or more well developed.

e. Advancement. The opportunity for advancement is displayed. Advancement comes as a result of skills development. Applying the concept of linear career development, the employer may embody advancement in a series of positive promotions to the positions directly above in the company's organization chart or changing to a larger company in which the same job includes broader responsibilities and more power. Inherent in this perspective are the thoughts that each job promotion is another step toward the top, along with more responsibility, more authority, and usually more salary.

In some professions, advancement cannot be measured in terms of linear career development or promotions. Artists, authors, opera singers, actors, teachers, doctors are examples of people in professions who must measure performance and advancement in other ways.

Regardless of the device used for measurement, the high achiever wants and needs a feeling of opportunity for advancement based upon performance.

The factors which will motivate employees and the factors which are the causes of employee dissatisfaction are not identical. Unfair company policy and administration, poor style of supervision, poor working conditions, lack of positive relationship with co-workers or supervisors, low salary or status, and lack of security in the job are examples of employment aspects which can cause dissatisfaction among employees. However, these same aspects, even when corrected, will not necessarily insure a positive work environment, even though a negative environment is removed.

As one reviews the list of high achievers' needs and the company environment necessary to satisfy those needs, it becomes apparent that the critical link in implementing the process is the supervisor.

9. Study a Company's Practice in Encouraging Career Development

Company policies and programs play an important role in creating a work environment which will be conducive to a high achiever, but management style of the supervisor can make company policy an impotent statement or complement it to such a degree that the high achiever will perform and thrive as a happy and productive person.

A review of management was recently conducted within the audit and accounting department of a large bank.

A new manager had assumed responsibilities in that department two years earlier. After that, a radical increase in employee productivity and in promotions had been observed. Before the new manager's arrival, the department had been a depository for problem employees. At the time of the survey it was regarded as one of the best places to work in the bank. The new manager was rewarded with a new title—vice president. Why? How?

The new manager's philosophy was that employees want opportunities to be promoted and to become more competent. This boss believed in the concept that career development is actually skills development and that job promotions come as a result of skills development. So the new manager had to design and use a management style which integrated career growth opportunities with daily work assignments. The design worked.

This style of management has six characteristics:

a. Exposure to many supervisors. Several project teams were developed with members from several departments of the company. Each team had a separate supervisor; however, each person was a member of several project teams. This approach enabled a person to learn about the range of skills needed within the many parts of the company and to understand the varied personal prejudices, pet theories, and work expectations of many managers. Armed with the data, the employee had a better idea about which skills to develop and how to use them. The benefits included an awareness of the differences of supervisors' expectations and a feeling of contact and participative pride with the operations within the department. Along with these is the chance to be seen and acknowledged by more of the supervisors and the opportunity to exhibit personal and professional skills.

Employees develop an accurate awareness of the most desirable skills because of the contact with a broad range of supervisors.

b. Supervisor-employee openness. Communication is necessary to make work flow more expeditiously and to create trust and understanding in the supervisor-employee relationship. The employee needs to know what the supervisor is thinking and expecting to assure harmony and unity of purpose.

Supervisors in this bank regularly spend time discussing departmental assignments as well as employee job assignments with the employees. Sharing in the concerns of the supervisor and understanding their responsibilities creates a mutual feeling of respect and trust. The supervisor receives additional input to be used in decision making and the employee gains more exposure to people higher up in the management hierarchy. The information and understanding will be used by the employees to guide and focus their own career skills development. Career decisions are now being made with factual data rather than with assumptions, gossip, or personality issues as a basis.

c. Continuous feedback. Immediate, continuous feedback sessions enable the employee to learn because they are specific and relevant to a current or recent action. The classical yearly salary review accompanied by the 15-minute talk with the boss is of little value because it is necessarily a series of the boss's value judgments made with several generalizations as the basis. Continuous feedback allows a focus on specific issues with concrete examples and incidents. These sessions relate facts instead of generalizations and result in conclusions instead of vague judgments.

d. Skills growth through team assignments. Work projects are assigned to teams which are made up of highly skilled, experienced employees and of those who are unfamiliar and untried in the type of assignment. Both parties experience growth. The untried employees develop new technical skill while the experienced individuals benefit by having to assess the team members' current skills and by structuring an efficient learning experience.

e. Team employee performance reviews. The group of supervisors which work with the individual is assembled to compile a report which will be used as the employee's performance review. The key to success in performance reviews is that they be in consonance with the employee's perception of what the review should say. A report which disagrees with that perception, regardless of whether the perception is accurate or inaccurate, may result in a feeling of injustice and thus have a negative effect upon career growth and skills development.

More factual input will be available when the group of supervisors is assembled for the evaluation. Fairness and objectivity may surface more easily. The continuous feedback concept is functional inasmuch as the employee should already know each supervisor's opinion of his/her work. The group evaluation focuses upon performance, retards the influence of a single supervisor's personal bias, and is perceived favorably by the employee.

f. Manager's philosophy. Consistent effort in developing new skills is the most rapid road to career development for the employee. As development occurs, the manager grows along with the subordinate in terms of influence and status. Losing a subordinate to another department through promotion can be a positive experience because a new opening is created in the department which can be filled by promotion. The manager's influence is now spread to that corner of the company where the former subordinate has assumed responsibility.

10. Accentuate the Positive When Considering a Job Change

The decision to change to Job B must be made because of the positive factors associated with Job B rather than the negative factors associated with Job A.

When several individuals were asked for the basis for their decision to accept a new position, the following responses were offered. Notice the total lack of comment about the desirability of the new job; rather, each response centers about the problems associated with the previous position.

"I had been at my previous job in the accounting department for over four years. In the beginning, the job offered lots of interesting things to learn and new people to meet. But then I had just stopped learning."

"The challenge had gone out of my job. I grew rapidly in our small company and I guess I topped out. Since I'm not a relative of the owner, I would never be a vice president in the company. Another thing, the job was not really fulfilling to me. When I look back, I don't feel I've accomplished anything significant. Nothing I can point to and say, *I did that!* Although I had worked on many projects within the company, I seemed to be a *helper* instead of the person who received the real credit."

"The field I worked in is undergoing atrophy. Some of the companies aren't dying, but they aren't growing either. When I looked above me in the company, I saw well-experienced, competent executives who were not getting promoted because the company isn't growing. I saw the handwriting on the wall. If I wanted to advance my career, I had to get out . . . the sooner, the better."

"More job responsibility is what I wanted. I'm 40 years old, experienced, well educated and a hard driving manager. Being ready for more responsibility and getting more are two different things. I just wasn't getting it there."

"Money is important to me; I use it (and so does society) as a measure of career achievement. Considering my professional skills, experience, and proven successes, I'm worth more money than I was being paid. I guess I was caught in one of those unfortunate situations where I'm worth more but the job I was doing isn't. Anyway, I think I wanted a job where I can make more money."

"Our company was imposing budget restrictions across the board. New departments were being dissolved; established areas were being trimmed. I was in the quality-control area. As our production volume slowed, our department was getting cut."

Further discussions and the responses indicated that each individual made the decision to change because of the negative factors associated with the Job A rather than the positive associated with Job B. If Job B does not happen to be the "right" job, another job change will be required, and another . . . and another until the right job does surface. The desirable job may never surface because the process outlined above does not focus upon evaluating and selecting a new job but rather upon leaving an undesirable current job. Use the following rule:

Change to Job B because the job offers

Opportunity for advancement.

Recognition for achievement.

Responsibility and authority for the job.

Environment for personal growth.

Summary

Practice the ten principles of career development:

1. *Influence sales and profits.*
2. *Know what a job is worth to the employer.*
3. *Develop your skills.*
4. *Select the right educational opportunities.*
5. *Develop the skills that the job requires.*
6. *Master the five traits that all employers look for.*
7. *Be a high achiever.*
8. *Identify the companies that encourage high achievers.*
9. *Study a company's practice in encouraging career development.*
10. *Accentuate the positive when considering a job change.*

6

*How to manage your
career by objectives:
Goal decision, action
plan, feedback*

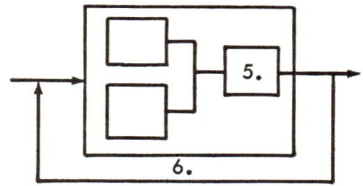

Management by Objectives

Your one-person service company is beginning to take shape. This chapter offers a step-by-step approach toward laying out your company. Chapter 2 presented the strategy. Chapters 3, 4, and 5 offered the key concerns in conducting the necessary analyses. With the information and judgments you so carefully developed, you are ready to take charge of your career and your future.

As we mentioned earlier, developing a plan is not enough. *Using* that plan to maximize your performance and to achieve your objectives is what you seek. Another proven business management concept can be applied to lay out your plan and then to make the plan work for you. It is called *management by objectives.*

Management by objectives (MBO) is a concept used by successful executives to increase operational efficiency. Its basis is the selection of a precise objective. Then, in light of the stated objective, a series of action plans are devised which will lead to the achievement of that objective.

87

During their implementation, the action plans are managed carefully to insure that the desired objective is being met.

For example, a company has decided to curb the growth of warehousing costs. The warehouse manager has now, as an objective, to lower warehousing costs. The approach toward achieving the objective may consist of the following:

Reduce the need for overtime wages paid to employees.

Refine ordering and scheduling procedures to make better use of time and quantity buying discounts.

Provide more frequent equipment maintenance to prevent major breakdowns.

Redesign warehouse layout to reduce wasted time and motions.

These four may be termed subordinate objectives; an "action plan" will be designed and used to achieve each. Achievement of the overall objective will be insured by monitoring the four action plans.

As you can see, this is a down-to-earth, uncomplicated approach to getting things done. And it works! It'll work for you.

Manage Your Career by Objectives

Management by objectives is the concept you will use in directing your efforts toward achieving career success.

The basis for using this concept is to have the career objective clearly in mind and well defined before taking any action. As the goal becomes more specific and well-understood, the sequence of jobs (subordinate objectives) are laid out. An important aspect of MBO is monitoring the progress toward each step and thus monitoring the progress toward the overall career objective.

Take these steps:

I. *Career objective:* Establish a career objective.

II. *Subordinate objectives and action plan:* Develop a sequence of jobs (subordinate objectives) which will lead toward the overall career objective; design action plans to be used in achieving each subordinate objective.

III. *Feedback:* Conduct constant reviews of progress toward each subordinate objective and toward the overall career objective.

To be effective, thus, this approach demands: using effective, decision-making strategy in establishing the goals; a total commitment to the goals; and frequent performance reviews.

I. Establish a Career Objective

Managing your career by objectives requires a well-defined career objective. Without a specific goal, there is no basis for determining the most efficient and productive course of action. If you don't know where you are going, how can you determine the best roads to take?

A generalization or vague statement of objectives is useless in applying a management approach to career development. Statements of objectives such as the following are too general to be useful: "I just want to be happy." "A position which would be challenging where I could make the most of my education and work experience." "A management position in a fast-growing, dynamic industry which offers great opportunity."

Stating your objectives is not a substitute for planning; rather, it is the basis for planning. Determining your objectives accomplishes the following:

Documents expectations.

Provides a firmer base for developing and integrating plans for personal growth.

Serves as the basis for feedback and evaluation.

Provides the basis for coordination and timing of career decision making.

Emphasizes the interrelationships of change, improvement, and personal growth.

As objectives increase in perceived clarity and become more specific, designating a career path will be highly facilitated.

The act of making a career selection is going to be an enjoyable and rewarding experience. You'll love doing it. It won't be as tough as you suspect. You're probably a little worried about your ability to reach this step and to do it with confidence and conviction. The task sounds a bit overwhelming, doesn't it! It won't be so.

Here's why. You will have conducted considerable research about career opportunities and about you. As more and more information is gathered, you are strengthening your ability to make the right decision. Prior to your research, you were being asked to make a decision without the information needed to evaluate the alternatives.

An example will illustrate what I mean. The little fellow in Figure 6–1 is faced with a decision: Should he invest his week's pay in the proposition where he might make $500 or he may lose the whole $100? He doesn't know how to evaluate the situation. What would you suggest to help him make his decision?

You might tell him that the probabilities associated with each outcome must be known before a decision could be made. No intelligent decision can be made with the information provided in Figure 6–1.

Figure 6–2 and Figure 6–3 illustrate the same situation but with probabilities assigned to the outcomes. Figure 6–2 offers a 99 percent chance of receiving $500. What do you suggest under these circumstances? Should he risk his paycheck?

Figure 6–1

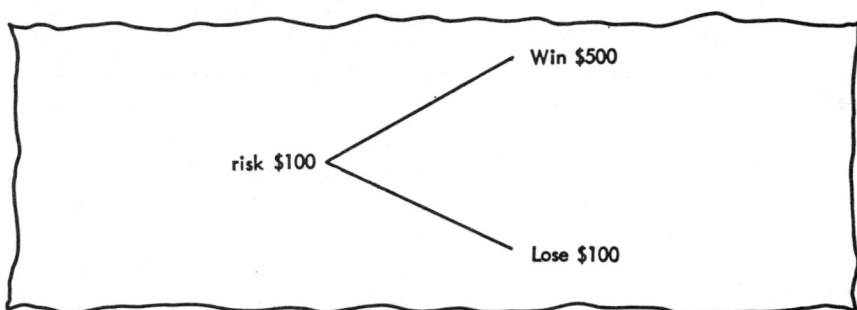

Figure 6–2

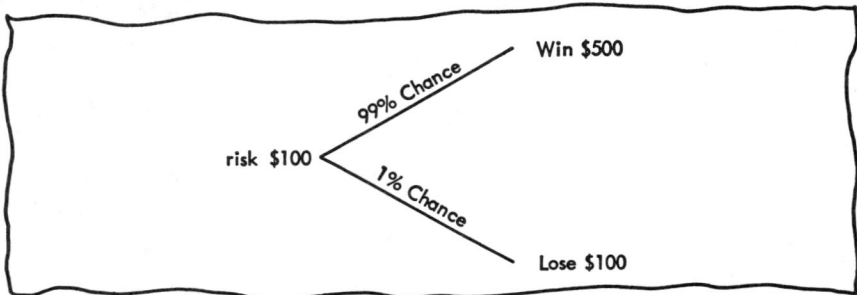

Figure 6–3

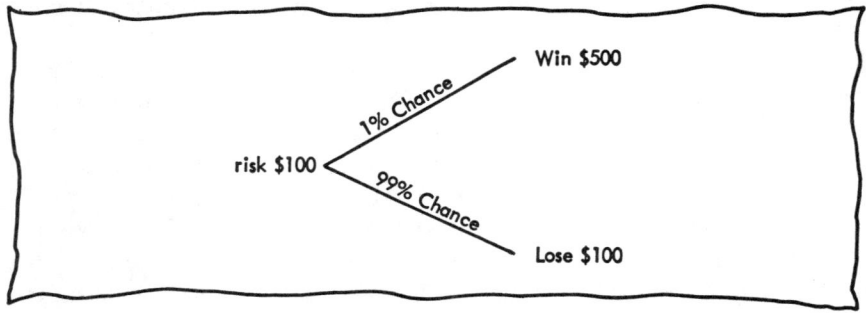

Figure 6–3 offers a less desirable situation; a 1 percent chance of receiving $500 and a 99 percent chance of losing the whole paycheck exists. What do you suggest here?

After you know how to evaluate a situation and know which questions to ask, an intelligent decision can be made—not before.

As you gather information, you are determining the probabilities for success in each career alternative. Knowing the facts will make your selection much, much easier.

However, you will be faced with a problem if your research is incomplete or slipshod. If this is the case, the decision will be more of a guess and you will lack confidence in the selection. Avoid uncertainty. Be thorough in your efforts. Here is how to do it.

A. Record the results of career opportunities research.

Your research has shown what is in demand today. Answer these questions.

1. What growth industries did you identify? (Name the three most promising, e.g., banking, data processing, transportation, health services.)

   a. _____

   b. _____

   c. _____

2. What company-types have the most potential within the growth industries?

	Industry A	*Industry B*	*Industry C*
Company-type	1. ____	1. ____	1. ____
Company-type	2. ____	2. ____	2. ____
Company-type	3. ____	3. ____	3. ____

3. Which job functions appear most promising in the areas identified?

   Job functions

   a-1_____

   a-2_____

   a-3_____

   b-1_____

   b-2_____

   b-3_____

c-1 _____

c-2 _____

c-3 _____

B. Record the results of personal resources research.

Your research has identified your resources. Which industry needs could you satisfy? Which of those opportunities fit you? Your chances for success will be maximized when you select a position which is aligned with your strongest capabilities, is in consonance with your values, and is satisfying to your needs. Answer these questions.

4. What are your strongest capabilities?

_____

_____

_____

5. What values do you seek in work or occupation?

_____

_____

_____

6. What of your personal needs are to be satisfied through work or occupation?

_____

_____

_____

C. Identify the best match.

Look at Part A, the data you have compiled about industries, company-types, and job functions.

Now look at Part B, the information you have offered about your capabilities, values, and needs.

Do you recognize a match? If no match is evident between you and the first three industries, two options exist. Amplify your qualifications through additional training and education or look at the next three industries, and the next, and the next until the best match becomes apparent. Look for the following in identifying the match; you will be qualified to answer these questions only after you have completed the research work.

Is it an industry which has a good potential for growth?

Is the company-type well equipped to capitalize upon industry trends?

Does the job function represent the backbone activity in the company?

Would this career allow you to utilize your strongest capabilities?

Would this career be satisfying to your needs and in consonance with your values?

Use the data in Part A and Part B to substantiate each answer with fact.

Answer this question: What is your career objective? (Be specific.)

_____

_____

_____

_____

_____

_____

II. Develop a Series of Subordinate Objectives Which Lead to the Career Objective

How will you achieve the career objective? During the research of the industries and professions you have selected, a path to the top became apparent. The sequence of jobs and assignments which offers the fastest road to career success was uncovered.

Each job in the sequence can be termed a subordinate objective. Decide upon and specify these steps. Write out an action plan for achieving each subordinate objective. Each action plan:

Aids in the search for better, more efficient methods of accomplishing your career goals.

Develops a sound basis upon which to estimate time and experience required.

Uncovers and anticipates problems to accomplishment.

Provides an opportunity to test the feasibility of the goals.

Determines the personal skills and economic conditions required to accomplish the goals.

Answer the following question.

What sequence of jobs will you pursue to achieve your career objective?

1. _____   4. _____
2. _____   5. _____
3. _____   6. _____

Now develop action plans for each job in the sequence. Answer the following questions.

What capabilities will you be required to develop for each of the steps?

1. _____
2. _____
3. _____
4. _____
5. _____
6. _____

What additional qualifications must you develop for each step? (Master's degree, years of experience, certification by state or professional societies and so on.)

1. _____
2. _____
3. _____
4. _____
5. _____
6. _____

What exactly are you attempting to achieve in each step as far as preparing yourself for the next step and in preparing yourself for the overall career objective?

1. _____
2. _____
3. _____
4. _____

5. _____

6. _____

What factors will you use to measure your performance in each step? (For example, abilities gained, promotions received, recognition, salary earned, and so on.)

1. _____

2. _____

3. _____

4. _____

5. _____

6. _____

What overall personal and professional achievements must you be able to exhibit to achieve the career objective?

_____

_____

III. Conduct Reviews with Feedback Information

Establish review programs whereby you will be monitoring progress toward each subordinate objective and toward the overall goal. Constantly reassess your activities and direction. Frequent reviews are associated with higher personal satisfaction and more consistent goal achievement.

Review your current subordinate objective at least four times each year (every three months). Use the report form offered in Figure 6–4.

Review your career objective at least yearly (every birthday). See Figure 6–5.

These reviews should also be conducted after every major incident in your life (marriage, birth of children, drastic change in personal financial situation, and so on) or in our economy (political, industrial, or social crisis).

To conduct these reviews you will need feedback information. Make every effort to get a constant stream of information about you and career opportunities. The sources will be the same you used in applying career decision strategy. They are: professional research groups, reading, memberships and programs, and references.

Figure 6–4
Subordinate goal review

1. What was my purpose in taking this job?

_____

_____

_____

2. How did I plan to fulfill that purpose?

_____

_____

_____

3. How do my actual achievements differ from what I had planned?

_____

_____

_____

4. What problems are arising?

_____

_____

_____

5. What do I plan to do to solve those problems?

_____

_____

_____

6. Should my purpose be changed?

_____

_____

_____

Two Ingredients for Success

The answers you provide for the questions in this chapter offer you half of the two necessary ingredients for *sure success* in anything you choose to do. These two ingredients are common factors in every, I repeat, *every* success story you have ever heard. Companies like IBM, EDS, Standard Oil, U.S. Steel, Ford Motor Company, and others were started and made successful by people like you—people who had those two key ingredients.

What are those ingredients? A solid idea and persistence.

Figure 6–5
Career goal review

1. What is my career goal?

_____

_____

_____

2. What factors did I use in deciding upon this goal?

_____

_____

_____

3. Have these factors changed? (Conduct a review of your capabilities, values and needs. Conduct a review of career opportunities.)

_____

_____

_____

4. How should my career goal be changed in light of the answer to question 3?

_____

_____

_____

5. Are my subordinate goals consistent with my career goal?

_____

_____

_____

6. How could my performance toward achieving the career goal be improved?

_____

_____

_____

The solid idea is what you are holding in your hand right now. It is the package of answers and approaches you have outlined in this chapter. It is the result of your research, your thinking, your analysis, and your deft application of the deductive reasoning process. You have identified a career pursuit, a plan for success that is a *solid* idea. Every fact is substantiated; none of your decisions were made as a result of a capricious cavort. What you have is a well-designed, well-documented approach toward achievement and self-fulfillment. You believe in it because you worked hard to develop it and because you know it is accurate.

Now for the second ingredient—persistence. Persistence is a state of mind which can be developed and cultivated. If you have persistence as one of your traits you have it because:

You have always had a definite purpose in mind as you approach any task. You know that a strong motive helps you to surmount any difficulty.

You really *want* to achieve your objective. You have the *desire* to win.

You shoulder the responsibility for your actions. Belief and trust in your own abilities empowers you to rely on yourself; you feel comfortable with that responsibility.

You are an organized person who extends the necessary effort to plan. You can take charge because you know what is supposed to happen.

You take the time to gather accurate information about any project you undertake. You function with knowledge, not guesses or suppositions.

From these seeds, grow the strengths necessary for persistence.

Extend yourself in performing the exercises outlined in previous chapters. The satisfaction you will enjoy with your decision will be directly proportional to the amount of work you have invested. Faith and trust in your results will be concomitant. A solid idea will be yours. Persistence will be easily developed (if it is not your trait now) because it grows from the five aspects we have outlined above (which are inherent in career decision strategy).

Summary

Manage your career by objectives. You will need to develop the following:
  I. *Career objective.*
  II. *Subordinate objectives and action plans.*
  III. *Reviews with feedback information.*
Career objective can be determined by taking these steps:
A. *Record the results of career opportunity research.*
B. *Record the results of personal resources research.*
C. *Identify the best match.*
Develop a series of subordinate objectives which lead to the career objective. Develop an action plan for each subordinate objective.
Conduct regular reviews with feedback information: use a quarterly report to review the current subordinate objective, and use an annual report to review the entire career plan.
Two ingredients for success are: a solid idea and persistence.

section two

Changing jobs versus staying put

How to know if you're ready for a job change

Causes for Unrest

The time may come when you'll come home from work one day, throw your coat aside, and head for the liquor cabinet. You'll be struggling with the ice tray and fumbling for a glass while you continue the muttering you started as you were driving home:

> That G_____ D_____ company, who do they think they are! And that boss of mine! He's so bad with people that it's incredible. He doesn't know about how to listen to people. All he does is give you his own ridiculous opinion. When you put a question to him, he dodges it by giving you an answer that usually has no relevance to the question. That's because he's incompetent and refuses to do anything about it. He's afraid of me so he keeps me and my ideas away.
>
> And another thing, that token raise I got this year! Who do they think they're kidding! Hasn't this company heard of inflation? I'm not even staying even.
>
> And when are those promises going to be coming true? At the beginning, they kept telling me about what a bright future they see for me here. Then, they keep putting me off with such statements as "when the opportunity arises" and "when the time is right" and "when we are sure you're ready."
>
> Well, I think I'm ready now. I'm ready for action, and I'm going to do something about it. . . .

Does any of this sound familiar? Have you ever felt like leaving the job, the boss, and the company in search of something better? If you have, you are not alone. Almost everyone has had some of the same feelings as outlined above at one time or another.

Are you really ready for a job change? Using the process of career decision strategy outlined in Chapters 2–6 will be your first step in answering this question. Apply the industry, company, and job analysis (described in Chapter 3) to your current employer. Match the results of your analysis to the information gathered about personal abilities, values, and needs. If your answer points to a job change, do it. Get started on a new career, new rewards, and more career satisfaction.

What if the result of your analysis confirms that you are currently in the right job for you? And, what if you still feel that you should change jobs? You may feel that you are in the proper industry and profession but the wrong company.

Before making the change, consider that you have invested much time and energy in getting to know your current job, company, and industry. A move may demand several months of starting from the beginning in building personal relationships within the new company, learning new technology, changing your residence, changing schools for your children, and a myriad of other considerations concomitant with such a change. Let's look closer.

What is it about your current job that causes your unrest? If you could identify the cause and deal with it successfully, the risks inherent in changing jobs would not have to be undertaken.

The most popular reasons for career and job changes are these:

1. No opportunity for equity participation.
    a. Employer has not offered participation.
2. Industry is becoming obsolete.
    a. Company has not attempted to plan against encroaching obsolescence.
3. Promotions unavailable.
    a. Too many well-qualified young executives.
    b. Too few new positions opening up.
4. Weak and indecisive leadership style.
    a. Incompetent boss.
5. Overbearing, self-centered leader.
    a. Refusal to delegate authority.
    b. No employee recognition for performance.
6. Personality differences.
    a. Lack of communication.
    b. Misuse of established formal and informal communication vehicles.
    c. Lack of regular employee performance reviews.

7. Unchallenging assignments.
    a. Company refuses innovation or risk of any kind.
    b. No chance for submitting company recommendations.
    c. Manager lacking skills and abilities necessary for company growth.
8. Unfair or immoral top management.
    a. Delegating responsibilities without the necessary accompanying authority.
    b. Promotions and salary favoritism shown to relatives and friends of top management.
    c. Broken promises.
9. Salary too low; reviews too few.
    a. Salary well below the average for similarly qualified individuals.
    b. Pay increases not commensurate with achievements.

Negotiation

One of the above may be the cause for your current state of career dissatisfaction. The question that now arises is, "How can each of these situations be handled to your benefit?"

Negotiation is the answer! Remember that *two* parties are involved: you *and your employer.* For you to benefit, your employer must perceive benefit too.

In his book, *The Art of Negotiating,* Gerard I. Nierenberg points out that negotiation is a cooperative enterprise and that common interests must be sought out. In a good negotiation, everybody wins. Negotiation is not a war or a game; no need for a winner *and* a loser exists. *Both* parties win in a successful negotiation.

Successful negotiators prepare by gaining an understanding of the other party's needs and that party's perception of those needs. If the negotiation arrives at a solution which includes the satisfaction of the other party's needs along with the satisfaction of your needs, you have most assuredly gained your objective by making it beneficial for the other party to grant your requests. An example from industry will emphasize our point:

Account 1: Need for lack of risk. An engineering firm, especially proficient in the construction of smelters, learned about a piece of land which had rich deposits of ore. The company also recognized that the owners lacked the necessary resources to remove the ore and to build their own smelters. Seeing this as an opportunity to help the owners while increasing the company's business and profits, executives of the company prepared a comprehensive and convincing presentation outlining their prowess in engineering construction. Several accounts of previously successful assignments were prepared. Cost projections for the development of the smelter were prepared. The company also made an exhaustive financial analysis of the income that would be realized by the owners because of the smelter.

When the presentation of these facts was made to the owners, the company emphasized two points: the company's ability to do the job and the benefits to the owners as a result of the smelter. The presentation was excellent, but the company did not get the job. The owners decided against building the smelter. Why?

The owners of the land did not believe in borrowing or indebtedness. They did not have on hand the necessary funds to pay the fee requested by the construction company. Even though they were convinced of the engineering firm's ability to do the job and of the potential income for their own company, they saw no way of financing the project from current resources and, therefore, rejected the company's proposal.

The engineering firm considered this an absurd decision. Why, they were practically handing the owners a multi-million dollar source of income for pennies! Then one of the wiser executives of the company recognized that they have two hands. He suggested that they approach the owners once again, but this time with both hands full. In one hand, the same presentation was offered, complete with its description of potential income for the owners. In the other hand was the promise to build the smelter at no cost to the owners in exchange for participation in the profits of its operation, if any. This new presentation, with both hands full, could not be refused. Both parties to the negotiation got their own way and maintained the concept of mutual benefit.

In other words, the company's initial presentation was based on the potential for profit when, instead, their presentation should have emphasized lack of risk and indebtedness. The owners perceived their need for lack of risk to be higher than their need for profit.

Another example will reinforce the importance of focusing upon the other party's perception. Keep in mind that selling is a form of negotiation.

Account 2: Need for convenience. A popular consumer goods manufacturer came up with a revolutionary product that would prove to be a boon to the busy parents of infants—a disposable diaper.

The product development team searched and researched the needed qualities in such a product. Their findings pointed out that the diaper should have the following characteristics:

1. *Comfort.* Their research findings determined the best size, shape, and texture of the materials to be used.

2. *Waterproof.* A plastic outer liner was recommended to retain moisture and to protect clothing and bedding.

3. *Protection against diaper rash.* The diaper construction was to in-

clude a layer of porous material which insulated baby's skin from the layers of moisture-absorbing materials.

4. *Convenience.* The diaper should have built-in adhesive tabs for applying the diaper without pins to add to the convenience and fit.

The manufacturer then designed and produced a television commercial to demonstrate the diaper's four characteristics. The appeal didn't work. The advertisement did not produce the results hoped for by the manufacturer. Why?

Further marketing research pointed out that buyers were not concerned with the design, construction, and materials related to a disposable diaper. Nor were they concerned about its protection against diaper rash. Parents were primarily concerned with one factor: *convenience.*

The manufacturer then rewrote its advertisement with an emphasis on convenience. The results of this change in appeal were dramatic. Even though the product had a full range of advantages and positive factors, listing all of them in the advertisement proved to be less effective than listing just the information important to the prospective buyer.

In other words, if babies bought their own diapers, manufacturers should advertise that they will keep baby drier and more comfortable. However, parents buy diapers; so, manufacturers should advertise that disposable diapers would provide convenience for mom and dad. Thus, the manufacturer sold its diapers and the parents received convenience. Everybody wins.

Prepare to resolve the unpleasant situation with your current employer by applying the same principle of negotiation—mutual benefit.

The following common situations are described with recommendations for action:

No Opportunity for Equity Participation

Background. You have turned down several attractive job offers from other companies in the past few years. However, now, you have reached the position with your current employer where equity participation has been earned and is justly deserved. But, it hasn't been offered.

Before changing. Ask for it.

Refrain from having a desk-pounding scene where your ultimatum is thrust at your employer with the threat of resignation if your request is not met.

Instead, have *both* hands full when you make your presentation. In one hand, offer your request for equity participation and point out why you are justified in making the request. Use facts instead of personal opinion.

In the other hand, show how the employer can benefit from granting your request. A suggestion might be that you be allowed to buy into the company; this approach benefits the company by increasing its working capital and benefits you by being able to participate in company profits. Make them an offer which they cannot refuse.

Industry Is Becoming Obsolete

Background. You have watched your company's fight to stay alive become more difficult each year. The real reason is industry atrophy rather than company deficiencies. You are a smart investor. You realize that your career requires an investment more precious than money— time. You are considering a change where you can invest your time in a growth industry.

Before changing. Answer the following four questions:

1. Can the situation be turned around?
2. What would it take?
3. What are the chances of it happening?
4. What is the payoff for you if the effort is successful?

Your decision to negotiate should be based upon the facts gained. The last of the questions is the most important; the payoff had better be worth the effort.

Use the comprehensive list of questions outlined in Chapter 3 to analyze your industry and company. If the analysis points out that the "ship is sinking," face the facts and make your change.

Promotions Unavailable

Background. The company has enjoyed successful rapid growth and development in the past, but now growth has slowed. The company is overstocked with highly competent and relatively young executives. The company is unable to offer the promotion you are expecting and for which you are qualified.

Before changing. Look around the company for a new idea, a new product, or a new market. Maybe you can create the company growth and expansion needed to offer greater career opportunities.

For example, a young marketing executive worked for an organization which sold produce to food brokers. He felt his career progress to be blocked by a very successful immediate supervisor who was also a marketing specialist.

The young executive came up with the idea of starting a new division which would sell fruit directly to public schools for school lunch programs. The idea was well received by the company and he was appointed as head of the new division which proved to be highly successful. The lack of new openings problem was overcome to everyone's benefit.

Notice the "two-handsful" concept. The executive wanted a promotion; the company wanted more sales and profits. Both achieved their objectives.

Weak and Indecisive Leadership Style

Background. As the work load and demands accompanying the leader's job have increased steadily, the boss is becoming less effective and is no longer doing the job properly. Whether the situation is due to old age, ill health, or lack of competence, the time has come for a change in management for the good of the company and for you.

Before changing. Recognize that two parties are empowered to make an expeditious change in leadership within the company:

1. The boss through resignation.
2. The boss's immediate supervisor (board of directors, president, department head, foreman, or ?) through reassignment or firing.

Ask both parties about their view of the situation and about their immediate plans for change.

Launch your inquiries in a fashion which would reflect your interest and concern. Your purpose is to discover both parties' perceptions of their needs. Why isn't the boss retiring or leaving? Why doesn't the boss's supervisor do something about the situation?

When you have answered these questions, you will be in an excellent position to come up with a solution of mutual benefit—for you, for the leader, for the leader's supervisor. If no solution becomes apparent, make your move.

Overbearing, Self-centered Leader

Background. The boss has guarded and held closely the authority to make all decisions. Harboring a personal view as a self-made success and the reason for the organization's well-being, the boss has refused to delegate responsibility and authority or to let other's receive recognition. This technique of management has necessarily limited the organization's ability to grow and to make more openings available.

Before changing. Get away from the boss.

This type of person is threatened by fast-rising employees. The boss may feel insecure about his or her personal abilities and, thus, protects his or her own job by preventing others from developing the skills required for promotion.

Negotiation with the boss is not the answer, because your advancement is exactly opposite the boss's desires.

Explore the possibility of your transfer to another department within the company. Before asking for the transfer, understand that you can maintain a positive relationship with the department you are leaving by offering to help find and train your replacement. This approach will result in mutual benefit because the current boss will not be left with the task of replacing you.

If a transfer within the company will not offer the new opportunities, leave the company.

Personality Differences

Background. The relationship between you and the boss has become progressively worse. You seldom talk to each other and enjoy this communication less. You are not sure of the boss's opinion of you, but you definitely have a negative opinion of the relationship.

Before changing. A breakdown in a relationship or the development of negative feelings between employer and employee are often due to: a lack of communication, misuse of established formal and informal communication, or a lack of regular employee performance reviews.

Could one of these be the cause of the problem at hand in your company?

Maybe the company's management doesn't know about these deficiencies.

If it's lack of communication, tell the boss about your perception of the problem. Ask for both an informal and a formal communications channel to be established. Explain your need to know what is happening within the company's other departments and within your own. Suggest a regular meeting time for your group and a few alternatives (such as luncheons) which would allow informal discussions. Be sure to describe the benefits to the boss: better understanding of interdepartment activities, closer view of intradepartment procedures, reduced chances for rumors, improved employee moral, and so on. Offer to assist in organizing these sessions. If the channels of communication *are* established but are being misused, point out the problem to management. Include the techniques to be used in rectifying the situation.

Another source of personal unrest is caused by management's failure to let employees know where they stand. Measures of performance and techniques of performance review must be established. If these conditions are symptomatic of your current employer, bring attention to the matter at once.

Unchallenging Assignments

Background. The company seems dull and uninteresting. The pure challenge, fun, and enjoyment of your job is gone. You're not sure of the reason, but you've concluded that you must need a change.

Before changing. Ask yourself for the reason behind your feeling.

When a dynamic individual gets this feeling, it could be because the company is rigid, unimaginative, and unyielding to new ideas and new ventures. A few of the reasons might be:

Insecure president (refuses to take chances).

Board of directors fears innovation or change.

Impossible channels of communications; can't get your ideas across.

Incompetent management (which becomes indecisive and causes frustration for you).

On the other hand, have you prepared yourself for more challenging assignments? Have you compiled an impressive record of successfully conducted assignments? Have you pursued continued education and participated in company-sponsored training and management development programs? Does management know about these achievements?

If you *are* qualified, ask for a more challenging assignment using the following approach:

1. Design one or two or more jobs which would be attractive to you and beneficial to the company.
2. Plan for finding and training your replacement in the job you now hold.
3. Make your presentation with the concerns of management in mind.

Unfair or Immoral Top Management

Background. You have been delegated many rather impossible tasks along with strong talk about your obvious value to the company and praise for your reliability. Through your extraordinary expenditure of time and effort, these tasks always get completed; however, your achievements are not rewarded with substantial promotions and salary reviews.

Before changing. Recognize that you may be working for an unfair or *immoral* employer. This type of employer is characterized by the following reoccurring improprieties:

Delegating responsibilities without the necessary accompanying authority.

Promotions and salary favoritism shown to relatives and friends of top management.

Broken promises.

Unfortunately, if the employer realizes and continues to repeat these tactics, you will not be able to change the situation easily. Get out.

If you suspect that the employer is unaware that the company has been unfair, confront the boss with your concern. Oftentimes an employer will rely upon a dependable, productive employee repeatedly. Soon the word *repeatedly* becomes *constantly*. And this usually means a change in job description and change in level of responsibilities. Because all of this evolves slowly instead of a formal job change, an employer may be unaware of what has happened. Bring it to their attention.

Salary Too Low; Reviews Too Few

Background. Your pay increases have not been commensurate with the achievements you have made for the company. Your compensation level is substantially below the industry level for others with similar responsibilities.

Before changing. Maybe your dissatisfaction has not been recognized; it may not have occurred to the boss.

Prepare a report outlining the current salary range for executives with responsibilities similar to yours within your industry. Get the facts by calling executive search firms in your area; their data is up to date and will reflect geographic bias. Amplify these statistics with salary surveys prepared by professional associations or government agencies (consult your librarian for assistance).

Meet with your employer to discuss the match between your salary and the facts you have gathered.

Another concern, do you and your boss have the same view of what your job is?

Job descriptions have a tendency to evolve around your strengths and abilities. If your current range of duties and activities no longer matches your original job description, point out that your current salary is still based upon a job description which no longer exists. And show the reason not only for a raise but also a complete revision of your salary structure.

If your boss is not empowered to rectify the salary situation, do not bypass that office to go to the authorized person. Rather, work through your boss to gain support.

Summary

The most popular reasons for career and job changes are:
1. *No opportunity for equity participation.*
2. *Industry is becoming obsolete.*
3. *Promotions unavailable.*
4. *Weak and indecisive leadership style.*
5. *Overbearing, self-centered leader.*
6. *Personality differences.*
7. *Unchallenging assignments.*
8. *Unfair or immoral top management.*
9. *Salary too low; reviews too few.*

Techniques of negotiation can be applied to solve unpleasant situations.

The basis for successful negotiations is the concept of mutual benefit.

section three

Techniques of job search

8 | *How to use the five major sources of job leads*

Sources of Job Leads

Determining the best sources of job leads for you will depend upon the type of job you want and your qualifications.

The source of job leads you used last time may no longer be best if your job objective is different this time. The approaches that worked for your friend may not work for you because of the differences in objective and qualifications. There is no "one surefire source that works best everytime for everybody."

You've probably considered the following techniques at some time in your thinking:

Use a personnel agency or executive search firm.

Call the job placement office of your alma mater.

Respond to the job listings in the classified ads of the newspapers.

Alert your friends, associates, and former employers about your job search.

Mail unsolicited resumes to several hundred companies.

Although you may find that several of these sources and others may be of assistance in your search, you are looking for the *most effective source*. Do not sacrifice your time and energies in the "long-shot" sources; that will reduce your effectiveness in tapping the sources you know to be more reliable and worthy of your efforts.

An experienced executive seeking a job change may find an executive search firm to be the quickest avenue of job leads. Technical professionals affiliated with a highly specialized industry or job function may find that personal contacts or trade associations will be the most effective source of assistance in making a job change.

If you are a recent college graduate seeking your first job, the college placement office may be an excellent source of job leads. If you are after a position with one of the smaller firms or with a highly specialized organization or with companies which do not have a campus recruiting program, your college may be able to offer little assistance; in this case, a personal telephone and mail job search campaign may be necessary.

That's enough of these mind-polluting suggestions! Don't be influenced by someone else's guesses about what techniques "may" work. You decide.

On the following pages, the five major sources of job leads and their usage are explained. You decide which to use for achieving your objective. As you understand each source's process and purpose, you'll find it easier to design a job hunting campaign which will be both effective and efficient.

I. What Job Agencies Can Do for You

Can a job agency provide the services you want?

All job agencies are not alike; they differ greatly in terms of the type of customers served, method of operation, range of services, fees, and effectiveness. If you are considering an agency to help in your job search, the following explanations will provide the information you will need.

Four categories of job agencies will be discussed: employment agencies, executive search firms, executive career counselors, and special services firms.

A. Employment agencies

Employment agencies earn their compensation by referring qualified applicants to employers who have listed a position with the agency. The types of jobs handled by placement agencies vary widely according to industry, company type, and job function. Openings may range from clerk, receptionist, and warehouse worker to middle level management positions. Salaries will range up to $25,000 yearly. Few positions in excess of $25,000 will be handled by employment agencies.

As an employer submits information such as a description of the job to be filled and the desired qualifications in a prime candidate, the agency searches through its files for people who can meet the requirements. If no appropriate candidates are on file, a newspaper ad is placed to draw mailings and inquiries from qualified applicants. The resumes received are screened and then forwarded to the employer for further action.

If you were to walk into an employment agency seeking information about job openings, the following process would be conducted:

1. You will be screened by means of a brief interview or perusal of your resume to determine the match between your qualifications and the type of jobs handled by the agency. If a match exists, you will be asked to fill out an agency application.

2. Next, a more extensive interview will be used to gather more information about your work experience skills, education, and other "desirable qualities."

3. If the agency knows of a suitable job opening, you will be referred to the employer after a brief "grooming" session where you will be informed of the employer's selection criteria and told what to emphasize as you describe your qualifications to the employer in the interview.

4. If the agency isn't currently aware of a suitable opening, your resume will be placed on file, to be used when an appropriate position is listed with the agency.

Employment agencies are usually paid by the employer—not by the job seeker. However, a few agencies ask for all or part of their fee from the job seeker. Know the situation before you do business with an agency; it makes little sense to pay when most agencies are employer retained.

A crucial concept in using agencies efficiently is to relate your job objective to the agency in terms of the industry, company-type, and job function. Inform them also of your qualifications for the position. If you are undecided about your job objective or unsure of your qualifications, contacting an agency may be an ineffective use of your time. Agency employees are not career counselors; rather, they work as job brokers. Their employees may often be people who have limited career counseling ability.

When evaluating an employment agency's ability to help you, determine their familiarity with people within the industry you are after. Look for an agency whose recruiters are mature, experienced professionals who have developed high-level contacts within the industry of your interest.

Lists of job agencies can be compiled by using the yellow pages of the telephone directory in your city. As you read their advertisements, you will see that some agencies specialize in a certain field such as: finance and accounting related positions. Some agencies handle a full range of job types. A directory of private employment agencies is available by writing to: National Association of Personnel Consultants, 1835 K Street, N.W., Washington, D.C. 20006.

B. Executive search firms

Executive search firms are retained as consultants by employers. They are hired to fill vacant or newly created executive positions which generally pay $20,000 and over. Employers are charged a fee which is usually computed upon a percentage (25–30 percent) of the prospective employee's annual salary; the employee pays nothing.

The search firm meets with the employer to develop the job description, determine the necessary education and background for a desirable candidate, and identify likely sources of successful executives who would be prime candidates for the position.

The search firm then approaches and screens candidates to compile a list of referable prospects; the employer makes the final decision.

Ordinarily, executive search firms are seeking successful, well-qualified, experienced candidates to fill their assignments. They have earned the nickname "body snatchers" because of their practice of locating and luring promising executives away from other employers. If you are a recent graduate with little experience or your present salary level is well below $20,000, executive search firms are a poor vehicle of employment assistance.

If you are an experienced executive, you may wish to send a resume with a *short* cover letter to executive search firms announcing the fact that you are interested in considering a job change; some executive search firms maintain extensive files of resumes for easy reference. Executive search organizations can be found in the Yellow Pages of your telephone directory listed under "consultants, personnel" or under "employment agencies."

A comprehensive list of executive recruiters is available by writing to: Management Information Services, American Management Associations, 135 West 50th Street, New York, New York 10020.

If you plan to write to executive search firms, be sure that:

1. You can easily command a salary of $20,000+.

2. *Experience and achievements* are clearly explained in your correspondence.

3. Information about your job interest is provided in *specific terms* rather than "glittering generalities."

C. Executive career counselors

Executive career counselors are retained by job-seeking individuals; *they are not paid by employers.* Career counselors assist undecided executives in selecting career goals by means of aptitude, interest, and psychological testing and through personal counseling sessions.

If you retain one of the firms involved in executive career counseling, be prepared to pay a fee between $600 and several thousand dollars. The fee will depend upon the range of services rendered. Understand that these firms do not guarantee that you will procure a job; you are required to pay their fee regardless of the success of the services.

Their services usually include all or part of the following:

1. Analysis of your present career situation.
2. Identification of your strengths and weaknesses as evidenced by your work history and through formal testing.
3. Development of a realizable job objective which would be suited to you.
4. Composition of a resume.
5. Formulation of a job search campaign.
6. Assistance in salary negotiations.
7. Guidance in future career management and development.

Some of the services rendered may include: composing and printing resumes and accompanying cover letter, circulating the resumes and letters to prospective employers through the use of mailing lists and advertisements, administering aptitude and psychological tests to assist you in achieving self-awareness and to prepare you for this type of testing in the event that a prospective employer requires you to take the tests, and personal counseling sessions to deal with any personality deficiencies you may be exhibiting.

All of the above services may cost several thousand dollars. If only a few of the services are needed, charges will be levied in accordance with the combination of services desired.

If you have defined your career objectives, you may find career counselors to be a costly stop on the road to employment. You do not need their services. On the other hand, if an individual is unsure of his qualifications and goals, unaware of the processes used to achieve self-awareness, and uninformed of the techniques of job search, then, counseling is needed to offer the needed guidance and direction. The needed counseling may be available through your college or university *at no cost to you.*

If it becomes your decision to use one of the executive career counseling organizations, understand the following aspects before engaging their services:

1. Nature of the contract you will be asked to sign.
2. The exact cost to you.
3. The list of services extended to you for the agreed upon cost.
4. All promises and guarantees written into the contract.
5. The specific results guaranteed.

D. Special services firms

Many organizations exist which offer an array of special services to the job seeker.

1. Resume peddlers. This type of firm charges you a fee ($10–$100) to circulate your resume to companies who have job openings. Your resume *and several hundred others* are usually bound in booklet form and then mailed to the personnel departments of many employers. Oftentimes, your resume does not actually appear in the booklet; rather, a shortened synopsis of your background is included.

Some of these firms promise individualized mailings of your resume. Often, this is accomplished in a very haphazard fashion. Instead of addressing the correspondence to a specific company executive, letters are sent to "President" or "Personnel Department."

Another poor practice used is the sending of a form letter instead of an individually typed correspondence.

A serious disservice rendered by these firms is the mailing of resumes to executives and companies *which you had specifically requested not to contact*. Although this mishap may be an oversight due to poor administration control by the service, what will you do when *your current employer* receives a copy of your resume from a resume peddler?

2. Resume writers. Resume writing firms translate your educational background and work experience into a grammatically correct resume. Sometimes, you may encounter a writer who actually knows about your profession and can write a resume which would be of real help to you in your job search. Unfortunately, most are merely good *word technicians;* little industry insight is offered.

Another drawback is apparent in the fact that all resumes generated by a resume writing firm may look alike. Vocabulary, layout, and composition may be easily identifiable and associated with the firm by seasoned personnel directors and search firms. As a result, the veracity and reliability of the content may be questioned if "overstatements" have been used regularly by the resume writing firm in the past.

3. Personal agents. Personal agents offer assistance in any needed variety of job search services including acting as a walking/talking promotional campaign for you. They, as a third party, talk up your "glowing capabilities" and "amazing achievements" to prospective employers in exchange for a fat fee from you *regardless of the success of the job campaign.*

4. Refundable fee type agency. This type of firm charges you a fee ($400–$800) to launch a job campaign for you. When you accept a position with an employer as a result of their efforts, the fee is returned to you in full. The agency gets its compensation by charging the employer for making the match.

Before you register with such a firm, find out what happens to your money if you locate a position without their services while you are registered with them.

II. How to Establish and Use Personal Contacts

Personal contacts are the primary source of job leads for upper level positions.

Identify friends and acquaintances who are involved with the industry you have selected. They can offer assistance in your job search by informing you of job openings as they occur. Since you cannot be in more than one place at a time, use these contacts as a research team to canvass the job market for you.

The efficacy of this approach will depend upon:

a. Selecting those contacts who actually know the chosen industry and the people within the industry.
b. Selecting contacts who are sincerely interested in helping you.
c. Informing the contacts about the object of your search *and* your qualifications for the position.

Examples of personal contacts to be explored will be: former teachers, business associates, community leaders, former employees, relatives, and friends who may be affiliated with the industry of your choice.

Friends and acquaintances who have recently changed jobs are a good source of information; they can offer insights into the processes that worked for them. Also, they can tell you about the jobs they found to be available.

Maybe you know of a person like yourself who is currently searching for a career opportunity. Exchange information about leads, sources, and companies; you will both benefit.

Look to your old appointment book and business card file to refresh your memory about possible contacts; you will find this to be an excellent source of ideas and company names.

Developing new contacts should be pursued constantly. Many executives have procured their present job through hard work and effort, through skillful use of abilities in executing their assignments, *and through a friend or acquaintance who informed them of the job opening.* You have heard the refrain, "He just happened to be in the right place at the right time." Another favorite is "Some people are just born lucky." An individual can put himself in the right place at the right time; he can also arrange to be lucky.

Approaches used to develop new personal contacts include:

1. Membership in professional societies. Select societies related to your field of interest and active in your geographic area. *The Encyclopedia of Associations,* Volume I, *National Organizations of the United*

120

Figure 8-1

The following lists of organizations are available in the *Encyclopedia of Associations,* volume I, National Organizations of the United States

1. Trade, business and commercial organizations.
2. Agricultural organizations and commodity exchanges. Includes agribusiness, animal breeders, conservation, forestry, fruit and vegetable growers, livestock and poultry producers, nurseries, research.
3. Legal, governmental, public administration and military organizations. Includes city, county and state administration, civil defense, employment security, federal government, housing and redevelopment, legal and legislation, planning, police, property rights, taxation.
4. Scientific, engineering and technical organizations. Includes aerospace, anthropology, architecture, astronomy, behavioral sciences, biology, botany, chemistry, demography, ecology, electronics, environmental quality, genetics, geology, information processing, meteorology, nuclear physics, oceanography, paleontology, parapsychology, phenomena, psychology, standards, water resources.
5. Educational organizations. Includes accreditation, administration, admissions, adult education, alternative education, black students, cooperative education, counseling, curriculum, extension education, financial aid, foreign students, gifted children, graduate schools, humanities, independent colleges and schools, integration, international exchange, junior colleges, research, retired teachers, scholarship, special education, technical schools, testing, urban schools.
6. Cultural organizations. Includes American studies, antiquities, architecture, art, artists, arts and letters, authors, black culture, books, broadcasting, comic art, composers, crafts, dance, Esperanto, folklore, history, human development, Indian art and history, librarians and libraries, medieval studies, motion pictures, museums, music, philosophy, poetry, theatre, world notables.
7. Social welfare organizations. Includes abortion reform, adoption, aging, alcoholism, anti-poverty, community action, correction, crime and delinquency, drug abuse, employment, family life, handicapped, homosexuality, housing, migrant workers, planned parenthood, population, recreation, relief, safety, selfhelp, sex information, service clubs, social work, suicide prevention, volunteerism, youth services.
8. Health and medical organizations. Includes allergies, blindness, blood disorders, cancer, child health, deafness, dentistry, dermatology, donor programs, health insurance, hospitals, hypnosis, mental health, nursing, obstetrics, occupational medicine, ophthalmology, osteopathy, pathology, pharmacy, psychiatry, public health, radiology, rehabilitation, surgery, technology, therapy, veterinary science.
9. Public affairs organizations. Includes captive nations, citizenship, civil rights, community development, consumer affairs, economics, free enterprise, human rights, international relations, peace movements, political parties, refugees, special days, United Nations, world affairs.
10. Fraternal, foreign interest, nationality and ethnic organizations.
11. Religious organizations. Includes Catholicism, ecumenism, evangelism, Judaism, missions, Protestantism, religious education, religious reform, science and religion, spiritualism.
12. Veteran, hereditary and patriotic organizations. Includes genealogical organizations.

Figure 8–1 (continued)

---

13. Hobby and avocational organizations. Includes CB and shortwave radio operators, collectors and restorers, craftsmen, gardeners, gourmets, numismatists, pet breeders, philatelists, treasure hunters.
14. Athletic and sports organizations. Includes archery, badminton, baseball, basketball, boating, bowling, boxing, camping, curling, fencing, fishing, golf, hockey, horse racing, lacrosse, rodeo, rowing, skating, skiing, soccer, squash, surfing, swimming, tennis, track, trail riding, underwater exploration, volleyball, wrestling.
15. Labor unions, associations and federations.
16. Chambers of commerce. Includes national, bi-national, and international.
17. Greek letter and related organizations. Includes federations and associations, Greek letter and non-Greek letter organizations (social, professional, and honorary).
18. Missing organizations list. Includes organizations, previously listed, which can no longer be located but about which no definite information concerning their status has been received. Organizations which have not responded to a questionnaire for at least three editions are also included in this section.

States offers a quite complete listing of national organizations from various industries, professions, and fields of interest. The table of contents is offered in Figure 8–1 to acquaint you with the type of listings included. Many of the organizations may maintain job placement services or offer job leads within the field of interest. Membership with the organization of your choice will acquaint you with men and women working in your field.

2. Writing articles for professional journals. If a professional journal exists in your field, write to the editors for information about the procedure to be followed in submitting articles. Ask for information about the type and style of articles preferred.

Companies and executive search firms use trade and professional journals regularly as a source for the names of experienced professionals.

3. Attending conventions. Conventions are an excellent spot to meet and develop relationships with people from a well-diversified list of geographic locations, all of them involved in your field of interest.

In the future, they may have you in mind when a search is being conducted or are asked for a referral to fill a position well suited for you.

You will also find executive search people attending these conventions as they seek qualified candidates for their clients.

4. Former colleagues and employers. Maintain your relationship with former colleagues and employers if they relate to your present and future fields of endeavor. A periodic phone call and an occasional luncheon will keep your name fresh in their mind. As they become aware of job opportunities or are approached by executive search firms for referrals, your name will be quickly brought to mind.

5. Civic organizations. Civic organizations such as the chamber of commerce will have a membership composed of active business leaders within the community. These dynamic individuals may be aware of job openings within their own company or with the company of one of their fellow members. The organization may also publish a regular newsletter where job openings may be found.

The above suggestions will assist you in getting exposed and recognized. Whether you are presently an executive or a student, regardless of your desires to procure a first job or make a career change—get involved *now*. Build a path for the future.

Take care not to misinterpret the get involved advice. Channel your activities such that they will complement your career plans. Don't spread yourself too thin!

III. How to Personalize Direct Mail Campaigns and Get Results

You have probably considered making up a voluminous list of companies and then flooding the countryside with copies of your resume. All in the hope that some companies must be looking for a person just like you, you would purchase stamps and envelopes by the gross and spend hours at the Xerox machine preparing copies of your cover letter and resume. Then you hope to sit back and wait for the mailman to lug in the bags of replies.

Don't do it! At least, not that way.

A form letter and a mass-produced, generalized resume mailed to "Dear Sir" at XYZ Company will usually get as a reply, a generalized form letter from the personnel department thanking you for the resume and informing you that it has been filed away safely.

A direct mail job search campaign can be of great assistance in locating the right position if you have done the necessary preliminary research:

a. Know about the company, the job title used by the company to describe the position you are seeking, and the name and title of the employee responsible for hiring in that part of the company.

b. Be aware of the selection criteria used by the employer to identify a qualified applicant for the position you are seeking.

c. Armed with this knowledge, you will be able to write to a specific individual with a personalized cover letter and resume which would emphasize those aspects of your abilities and qualifications which would (coincidentally of course) exactly match the job title and selection criteria used by the employer.

This approach will get *results*.

Where will you get the company information you will need? Call or write to the company and ask for it.

Compile a list of companies, organizations, and professional associations affiliated with your field of interest. Call or write to company representatives and *ask for the preliminary information you desire.* You will then be equipped to design a mailing which will get the results you want.

After your preliminary research is completed, launch the mailing according to these important instructions:

1. Compile the list of companies carefully; be sure that all the companies have the type of job or opportunity you are seeking.

2. Address the correspondence to a specific person—the person who is in charge of the department in which you would like to work. Never send a correspondence to "Vice president—Finance" or "Personnel Department."

3. Know the selection criteria used to identify desirable employees in your field; get this information by asking employers directly. Insure that your correspondence emphasizes those of your qualifications which fit the selection criteria.

4. Follow up each of your mailings with an analysis of what got results and what did not.

Appendix A will help in compiling your lists of companies and associations.

IV. Identifying Publications Related to Your Field of Interest

Publications may provide a fertile source of job leads.

Newspapers from major cities have extensive career opportunity listings on weekends. These openings will be for experienced people seeking positions up to the middle management levels. Since many employers do not list their company name, applicants are requested to send a copy of their resume to a post office box number. In these cases, an outstanding resume and a cover letter will determine your chances for an interview.

Use back issues of newspapers (2–3 months) as well as recent editions. Oftentimes management jobs are not filled readily; you may be applying just as the company has exhausted its willingness to look at additional applicants.

Newspapers can be used in another fashion. Review the financial section to see who has been promoted (you may qualify for his job), what companies have been acquired, merged, expanded, and so on. This is a good technique to discover where the action is. Look for notices about companies which are moving into your area or are establishing new branch offices or divisions.

Trade publications and periodicals offer the latest information about their industry and the most dynamic companies operating within the field. Figure 8–2 offers a list of trade periodicals by industry or profession.

Figure 8–2

Periodicals and publications grouped by industry or profession

Accounting
  The Accounting Review
  The CPA Journal
  The Journal of Accountancy
  The Journal of Taxation
  Management Accounting
  Taxes
Advertising
  Advertising Age
  Bill Board
Automotive and mechanical equipment
  Air Conditioning, Heating and
    Refrigeration News
  Automotive Industries
  Heating, Piping & Air Conditioning
Banking
  Banker & Tradesman
  The Bankers Magazine
  Bankers Monthly
  Banking/Journal of the American
    Bankers Association
  Federal Reserve Bank of New York
  Federal Reserve Bulletin
  First National City Bank
  Journal of Commercial Bank
    Lending
Broadcasting
  Broadcast Engineering
  Broadcasting
Building materials and construction
  Architectural Record
  Concrete Products
  Construction
  Construction Bulletin
  Construction Digest
  Construction Equipment
  Construction News
  Construction Review
  Construction Specifier
  Constructioneer
  Constructor
  Contractor Magazine
Chemicals, drugs, and allied products
  American Druggist
  Analytical Chemistry
  Chemical & Engineering News
  Chemical Equipment
  Chemical Marketing Reporter
  Chemical Week
Data processing
  Computer Design
  Data Management

Data Processing Magazine
Datamation
Electrical machinery and equipment
  Circuits Manufacturing
  Electrical Construction &
    Maintenance
  Electrical World
  Electronic News
  Electronic Servicing
Engineering
  Assembly Engineering
  Civil Engineering-ASCE
  Control Engineering
  Engineering News-Record
  Marine Engineering/Log
  Materials Engineering
  Mechanical Engineering
  Package Engineering
  Plant Engineering
  Power Engineering
  Power Transmission Design
Finance
  Barron's
  Business Week
  Credit and Financial Management
  Dun's
  The Economist
  Financial Analysts Journal
  Financial Executive
  Financial World
  Forbes
  International Monetary Fund
  The Journal of Finance
  Nation's Business
  Organization for Economic Co-op-
    eration & Development Observer
  The Review of Economics and
    Statistics
  Trusts & Estates
Forest products
  Forest Industries
  Southern Lumberman
Food and beverage processing
  Bakery Production & Marketing
  Brewers Digest
  Canner/Packer
  Food Engineering
  Food Processing
  Food Technology
  Meat Processing
  Progressive Grocer
  Quick Frozen Foods

Figure 8–2 (continued)

Glass, paper, and packaging	Merchandising (retail and wholesale)
Food & Drug Packaging	Chain Store Age, Executives Edition
Modern Packaging	Journal of Retailing
Packaging Digest	Merchandiser
Paper, Film & Foil Converter	Stores
Paper Trade Journal	Metals and metal products
Paperboard Packaging	Iron Age
Pulp & Paper	Mining
Health care and products	Coal Age
Health Care Product News	Coal Mining & Processing
Hospitals	Rock Products
Medical Economics	Personnel administration and industrial
Modern Hospital	relations
Modern Medicine	Industrial and Labor Relations
Insurance	Review
Best's Review Life/Health	Labor Law Journal
Insurance Ed.	Personnel
Best's Review Property/Liability	Personnel Journal
Insurance	Public Relations Journal
Metropolitan Life Insurance	Petroleum and allied products
Company	Fuel Oil/Oil Heat and Solar Systems
The National Underwriter Life &	National Petroleum News
Health Insurance Edition	Oil & Gas Journal
The National Underwriter Property	Petroleum Engineer International
& Casualty Insurance Edition	Pipeline & Gas Journal
Management	Pipe Line Industry
Administrative Management	World Oil
Administrative Science Quarterly	Publishing
Harvard Business Review	Editor & Publisher
Industrial Management	Graphic Arts Monthly and the
Management Review	Printing Industry
Management Science/Journal of the	Publishers Weekly
Institute of Management Sciences	Real estate
Operations Research	Appraisal Journal
Supervisory Management	Land Economics
Manufacturing	Progressive Architecture
Industrial Development and	Transportation
Manufacturers Record	Aviation Week & Space Technology
Industrial Research	Railway Age
Industry Week	Railway Track & Structures
Production	Utilities
Textile World	Electric Light & Power
Marketing	Public Utilities Fortnightly
Industrial Marketing	Telephone Engineer & Management
Journal of Marketing	Telephone
Journal of Marketing Research	Water & Sewage Works

Consult your librarian for information about directories, handbooks, and reference volumes which may serve your needs. Review Appendix B for a comprehensive bibliography of helpful directories, handbooks, and references. See Figures 8–3 and 8–4 for additional ideas.

Figure 8–3

Examples of reference volumes which can be used to identify sources of job leads

If you wanted a career in management consulting:

American Management Association. *Directory of Consultant Members* (annual).

Association of Consulting Management Engineers. *Directory of Membership Services*.

Association of Management Consultants. *Directory of Membership and Services*.

Wasserman, Paul, and W. R. Greer, Jr. *Consultants and Consulting Organizations*. New York Graduate School of Business and Public Administration, Cornell University.

If you wanted a career in portfolio management:

Money Market Directory. New York: Money Market Directories, 1971. A directory of 4,600 institutional investors and their portfolio managers. Includes assets for each. Part 1 covers "Tax-Exempt Funds" (pension funds, endowments, foundations); Part 2, "Investment Services" (banks, insurance, investment services, Canadian and foreign operations). Both are listed geographically with alphabetical indexes.

If you wanted funds to launch you in starting your own business:

Venture Capital. New York: Technimetrics, Inc. A directory of corporations and partnerships that make high-risk funds available to businessmen. Indicates area preferred for investment, approximate range of financing, most recent venture capital investments.

Figure 8–4

Reference volumes listing individuals who may know of job openings within their industry

American Men and Women of Science; The Social & Behavioral Sciences. 12th ed. New York: R. R. Bowker Company, 2 volumes.

Dun & Bradstreet, Inc., *Dun & Bradstreet Reference Book of Corporate Management* (annual). Brief biographical information about top executives, arranged by company. Includes an alphabetical index by executive's name.

Who's Who in Advertising (biennial).

Who's Who in America (biennial). Biographical data on prominent living Americans.

Who's Who in Banking: The Directory of the Banking Profession. 2d ed. New York: Business Press Inc.

Who's Who in Consulting: A Reference Guide to Professional Personnel Engaged in Consultation for Business, Industry and Government. Ithaca, New York: Graduate School of Business and Public Administration, Cornell University.

World Who's Who in Finance and Industry. Career sketches of leading business executives and others noteworthy in the fields of finance and industry. A selected index by company is at front. Biennial.

The chamber of commerce in your county may publish a directory of businesses in the area. For example, the *Business Directory and Buyers*

Guide published by the Los Angeles Chamber of Commerce is designed to provide information on companies in Los Angeles, Orange, Riverside, San Bernadino, and Ventura counties. The directory includes: manufacturers, wholesalers, distributors, retailers, manufacturers agents, hotels, services, transportation, communications, utilities companies, construction firms, financial institutions, insurance and real estate firms, agricultural, and extractive industries.

IV. How to Use College Campus Recruiting Offices Properly

If you are a student or recent graduate, the campus may be of assistance to you in meeting with employers.

Each semester, thousands of companies send recruiters to college campuses to interview prospective employees. These companies are primarily seeking recent graduates with little or no work experience. The job openings are generally trainee, introductory level, or development program positions. Organizations recruiting on college campuses to interview graduates for executive positions in middle or higher management jobs are very few.

Companies who send recruiters to campuses regularly tend to be large organizations which exhibit an ongoing need for new employees; companies will generally concentrate their recruiting within the geographic area of the job opening.

Therefore, on-campus recruiting may be a poor approach to job search if:

a. You are well-experienced in the field you wish to work.
b. You are seeking a position very distant from your college or in a foreign land.
c. Your objective is to find a small-or medium-sized company.
d. Your field of expertise is very specialized.

In each of the above cases, a personal job search campaign will prove most helpful. While on-campus recruiting may turn up the opportunity you want, the chances are slim.

If you decide that on-campus recruiting will be of assistance, avoid the common mistake made on campuses throughout the country: Since on-campus interviewing is so convenient, the danger is that students register for 15 or 20 interviews with varied types of industries and companies before each company has been researched and evaluated for a match with their career objectives. The interviewing sessions actually turn into an information session for the students while the company representative is unimpressed because of the student's lack of seriousness and preparation. The student has impaired his chances for employment with the company by making a poor initial impression.

Students who make use of on-campus interviewing in a serious manner, after the necessary preliminary research and evaluation has been made, find themselves to be highly sought after.

If you are an experienced alumni seeking a job change, your alma mater may be equipped to offer a job referral service. The quality and range of services will vary greatly from school to school.

Inform the placement director about the type of position you are seeking. You will be told about the chances for such referrals through the placement office.

Summary

Identify the most effective sources of job leads by considering the job you are seeking and your qualifications.

Types of job agencies include: employment agencies, executive search firms, executive career counselors, and special service firms. Employment agencies work primarily with candidates who earn under $25,000. Executive search firms are retained by employers; they work with people in the $20,000+ category. Executive career counselors are paid by the job-seeker; a job is not guaranteed as a result of their services.

Personal contacts will be of greatest assistance when: you select contacts who actually know the industry and the people within it, the contacts are sincerely interested in helping you, you offer your contacts complete accurate information about the object of your search and your qualifications for the position.

Participation in professional, social organizations and clubs offer a means of meeting leaders in their respective areas and professions.

Direct mail campaigns can be effective if you have researched the companies and their selection criteria before sending letters and resumes.

College campus recruiting is conducted primarily by large companies seeking new or inexperienced graduates.

Periodicals and reference books offer good sources of company information.

9 | *How to write a resume which will make an employer want* you

Purpose of a Resume

You are able to compose a resume which will make you stand out head and shoulders above all other applicants with similar qualifications. And employers want you to do it. How?

You do the thinking for the employer. As employers read your resume, they'll be trying to determine the application of your skills, achievements, and abilities to the job in question. Save them the trouble; write about your qualifications to show their applicability. This way, there's no chance that the employer will misinterpret or fail to see your suitability for the position.

The purpose of a resume is to get you invited to interviews. Put yourself in the position of an employer:

Would you make a job offer to a stranger who had mailed a resume to you unsolicited? No.

Would you make an offer of employment to an applicant sending a resume in response to your newspaper advertisement or job listing? No.

Would you present a job to a job seeker after receiving their resume from a mutual friend or acquaintance? No.

Would you employ any person merely on the basis of reading their resume? No.

Job offers are extended only after interviews; therefore, the purpose of the resume in conducting a job search is to get you invited to interviews.

Your resume will get you invited to interviews everytime it is sent out if it shows the employer that you are able to satisfy one or more of the company's needs. Simple concept isn't it? You will identify the company's needs and then display your qualifications and their application to the job in question.

Allow me to revert to the classics for emphasis.

Account 1: The year is 1826. Put yourself in the place of Emperor Francis II of Vienna. You're looking for a qualified music master for the post of assistant conductor at the Imperial Court of Vienna.

You receive this letter:

Your Majesty!
Most gracious Emperor!

With the deepest submission the undersigned humbly begs Your Majesty graciously to bestow upon him the vacant position of Vice-Kapellmeister to the Court, and supports his application with the following qualifications:

(1) The undersigned was born in Vienna, is the son of a schoolteacher, and is 29 years of age.

(2) He enjoyed the privilege of being for five years a Court Chorister at the Imperial and Royal College School.

(3) He received a complete course of instruction in composition from the late Chief Kapellmeister to the Court, Herr Anton Salieri, and is fully qualified, therefore, to fill any post as Kapellmeister.

(4) His name is well known, not only in Vienna but throughout Germany, as a composer of songs and instrumental music.

(5) He has also written and arranged five Masses for both smaller and larger orchestras, and these have already been performed in various churches in Vienna.

(6) Finally, he is at the present time without employment, and hopes in the security of a permanent position to be able to realize at last those high musical aspirations which he has ever kept before him.

Should Your Majesty be graciously pleased to grant this request, the undersigned would strive to the utmost to give full satisfaction.

Your Majesty's most obedient humble servant,

Franz Schubert[1]

After reading this letter of application, are you moved toward meeting Mr. Schubert? Do you feel a strong positive urge to pursue this individual, to further discuss the job? Do you feel assured that he has the necessary qualifications for the position?

May I assume that your reaction is mildly positive. The candidate sounds interesting but not an overwhelmingly ideal individual. You would want to look at others also. Another situation is now offered for comparison.

---

[1] By permission from M. Lincoln Schuster, ed., *A Treasury of the World's Great Letters* (New York: Simon & Schuster, Inc., 1940).

Account 2: The year is 1482. You are Lodovico Sforza, the popular Duke of Milan. As your empire grows, you find the need for a stronger army and a more competent director of siege and defense.

You receive this letter:

Having,[2] most illustrious lord, seen and considered the experiments of all those who pose as masters in the art of inventing instruments of war, and finding that their inventions differ in no way from those in common use, I am emboldened, without prejudice to anyone, to solicit an appointment of acquainting your Excellency with certain of my secrets.

1. I can construct bridges which are very light and strong and very portable, with which to pursue and defeat the enemy; and others more solid, which resist fire or assault, yet are easily removed and placed in position; and I can also burn and destroy those of the enemy.

2. In case of a siege I can cut off water from the trenches and make pontoons and scaling ladders and other similar contrivances.

3. If by reason of the elevation or the strength of its position a place cannot be bombarded, I can demolish every fortress if its foundations have not been set on stone.

4. I can also make a kind of cannon which is light and easy of transport, with which to hurl small stones like hail, and of which the smoke causes great terror to the enemy, so that they suffer heavy loss and confusion.

5. I can noiselessly construct to any prescribed point subterranean passages either straight or winding, passing if necessary underneath trenches or a river.

6. I can make armoured wagons carrying artillery, which shall break through the most serried ranks of the enemy, and so open a safe passage for his infantry.

7. If occasion should arise, I can construct cannon and mortars and light ordnance in shape both ornamental and useful and different from those in common use.

8. When it is impossible to use cannon I can supply in their stead catapults, mangonels, trabocchi, and other instruments of admirable efficiency not in general use—In short, as the occasion requires I can supply infinite means of attack and defense.

9. And if the fight should take place upon the sea I can construct many engines most suitable either for attack or defense and ships which can resist the fire of the heaviest cannon, and powders or weapons.

10. In time of peace, I believe that I can give you as complete satisfaction as anyone else in the construction of buildings both public and private, and in conducting water from one place to another.

I can further execute sculpture in marble, bronze or clay, also in painting I can do as much as anyone else, whoever he may be.

---

[2] By permission from M. Lincoln Schuster, ed., *A Treasury of the World's Great Letters* (New York: Simon & Schuster, Inc., 1940).

Moreover, I would undertake the commission of the bronze horse, which shall endue with immortal glory and eternal honour the auspicious memory of the illustrious house of your father and of Sforza.——

And if any of the aforesaid things should seem to anyone impossible or impracticable, I offer myself as ready to make trial of them in your park or in whatever place shall please your Excellency, to whom I commend myself with all possible humility.

Leonardo Da Vinci

After reading this letter of application, what is your reaction?

I found myself crying out "Yes! Yes! Yes! Bring this man to me, at once! I want to meet him, to test his skills, to view his feats."

Why did the letter evoke this response? You and I realize that Da Vinci was a master of many arts and sciences; he was a biologist, engineer, geologist, botanist, artist, painter, sculptor, inventor, and prolific writer. However, his letter to the Duke of Milan emphasized only those skills relevant to the job to be done. And he described his skills in a most appropriate manner showing their application to war.

An excellent example is his statement, "I can construct bridges which are very light and strong and very portable, with which to pursue and defeat the enemy." Many applications exist for portable bridges, but Da Vinci describes them and their use in war.

The Duke could not possibly overlook Da Vinci's qualifications. If you felt moved to meet the person who wrote the letter, it had served its purpose—to get the applicant invited for an interview.

To satisfy your curiosity, Leonardo Da Vinci got the job and kept it for 16 years. Franz Schubert, a most qualified applicant for the job as Vice Kapellmeister, did not even receive acknowledgment of his letter much less an interview. Needless to say, he didn't get the job.

Necessary Information

Your first step in preparing a resume will be to gather the necessary information by doing the following:

1. Know your qualifications; complete the personal inventory, Appendix C.
2. Know the prospective employer's job description and selection criteria; complete the employer data form, Appendix D.
3. Rank your qualifications according to their ability to complement the employer's selection criteria; complete qualification ranking, Appendix E.

Don't make the common mistake of trying to write an effective resume without knowing about *both your qualifications and employer's selection criteria.* Unless you know what the employer is seeking, you will not be able to guide them in understanding the applicability of your qualifications to their needs.

If you had difficulty in completing Appendix D, you may find that you need more information about an employer. Ask for an "information session." Don't use a job interview to gather information.

A quite unique method of gaining the information is to call the company in question and ask for the answers.

Another often overlooked approach to gathering information about a company is to ask the company's major competitors for their observations. If you approach individuals and organizations openly, explaining that you are trying to understand their company's selection criteria, you will almost always be accommodated graciously. Become aware of the prospective employer's emphasis placed on professional achievements, education, grade point average, reputation of school, work experience, extracurricular activities in school and in personal life, communication ability, military status, professional awards and honors, references, and long-range career plans.

Although some components of the selection criteria may vary from person to person within the same industry, a definite sketch of the desired candidate will emerge.

Be sure that your job objective coincides with the job being offered.

Statement of job objective should be clearly specified in the initial portion of your resume. The remainder of the resume should be used to highlight those aspects of your achievements which qualify you for the position as stated. Focus primary emphasis upon those qualifications which have direct bearing on your job objective.

If you have not decided upon a job objective—including a description of the position you are seeking, industry desired, and type of company preferred—

YOU ARE NOT READY TO WRITE AN EFFECTIVE RESUME!!!

An individual who has formed no specific job objective may sometimes throw together a temporary resume which catalogs his background and achievements. The resulting resume is barely adequate and will be of very little assistance in job search.

Content of Your Resume

Display your qualifications with a purpose in mind—to get invited to an interview.

Offer information which is directly relevant to the employer's selection criteria. Do not flood the reader with too much data; your important qualifications will lose emphasis when surrounded by irrelevant minutia.

The following items of information are usually required by a prospective employer:

A. Identification

Necessary identification data will be:

a. Full name.
b. Address.
c. Telephone number including area code.

Omit information such as: height, weight, age, sex, race, religion, national origin, ancestry, and place of birth unless such information is relevant to the selection criteria.

B. Job objective

Your job objective is of critical importance. Information in the statement should include:

Job function desired—e.g., marketing research analyst, loan analyst, salesman, management consultant, investment analyst, store manager, etc.

Company-type—e.g., small, medium, large; sole proprietor, partnership, corporation; local, national, or international; manufacturer, distributor, retailer, etc.

Industry preferred—e.g., banking, farming, public accounting, insurance, aerospace, retailing, public utilities, government, construction, food distribution, etc.

Statement of objective should reflect your PRESENT or SHORT-RANGE plans; do not include your life goals.

The remainder of the resume should illustrate and emphasize your qualifications for the position described in the job objective. Therefore, list your most impressive qualification first; refer to Appendix E.

C. Education

If you are a recent graduate, education may be one of your strongest selling points. As employers read this section, they will be asking the following questions:

a. What did you study?
b. What skills have you developed?
c. How do these skills apply to the job in question?

Elaborate upon your major, courses taken, special assignments, term papers, research projects, and any information which seems pertinent to your job objective.

While it is important to be complete in listing your degrees and achievements, be sure to allow more space and offer more detailed information' to those facts which emphasize your qualifications for the job objective as stated.

D. Work experience

As the employers read this section, they will be asking the following questions:

a. What were your responsibilities?

b. What did you do to carry out these responsibilities?

c. What were the results of your efforts?

d. How does this apply to the job in question?

Emphasize and explain in detail those job assignments which most effectively qualify you for the stated job objective. If you received successively more responsible assignments, emphasize that growing responsibility. Make special note of a promotion or recognition as a result of success in a particular assignment.

DO NOT EXPLAIN THE COMPANY'S OPERATIONS OR YOUR DEPARTMENT'S RESPONSIBILITIES UNLESS THEY ARE NECESSARY TO MAKE YOUR JOB ASSIGNMENT MORE EXPLICIT.

Part-time and summer work experience may be handled in paragraph style by relating job titles only. More space or a more formal presentation is warranted when these experiences are pertinent to your job objective.

E. Extracurricular activities

Prospective employers review the section on extracurricular activities to get an indication of your outside interests, social awareness, desire to get involved, energy level, and leadership potential. Include activities such as professional activities, hobbies, club memberships, campaigns, awards, honors, and other personal interests.

Many jobs are especially fitted for a well-rounded individual. Having been chosen as a member by honorary groups or elected to professional societies in your field speaks well for your future in that field. Affiliation with social organizations, church groups, or community projects demonstrates social awareness. If your participation in any activities resulted in a special award or election to an office, this fact may be used to indicate your leadership abilities.

If you have little work experience, your extracurricular activities may be one of your stronger assets. Be sure to emphasize those extracurricular activities which enhance your qualifications for the stated job objective.

Employers realize that it is difficult to be involved in extracurricular activities if you had to work your way through school; in this case, lack of activities is not a liability. Instead, shift the emphasis of your resume to the work assignments, hours worked per week, and percentage of college expenses earned.

F. Military

Military record should be included in your resume if applicable.

A detailed description of your duties and assignments while in the service is suggested only if they are pertinent to your job objective.

G. References

Show that you are prepared to forward business or personal references to the prospective employer, if requested. If companies ask for references but do not specify the number desired, three should be sufficient: a professor, a former employer or service officer, and someone who can serve as a character witness.

H. Other

If you have additional information illustrating your qualifications, be sure to mention them. Examples of this type of information may be: information on personal background, foreign language ability, political achievements, publications, and so on.

Include this type of data only if the information is relevant and will enhance your qualifications for the desired position.

Physical Aspects of Your Resume

Your resume should be distinctive, impressive, and professional; it should look as well as be truly outstanding. Achieving the desired appearance will demand attention to detail.

An excellent key to follow in composing your resume is to use no technique or component which would switch the emphasis from the content.

Strive to achieve an appearance which would be complementary to the message being conveyed in the resume. Above all, it should be easily readable and in good taste.

A. Length

Short, concise, well-written resumes convey information more efficiently and are more easily understood and remembered than their longer counterparts. Even a well-experienced individual should not exceed two pages.

If you encounter difficulty in following this rule, perhaps you are trying to emphasize everything instead of just those factors which are directly pertinent to your job objective.

B. Paper

When choosing paper for your resume, consider the color, composition, and size.

White, grey, or beige paper are acceptable and in good taste. Brightly colored, striped or patterned paper are less effective because they are difficult to read and distract the reader.

Use a top quality paper for each copy of your resume. Bond, linen, or pebble textured finish paper are most preferred. You may choose from paper in the 20–50 lb. weight range to insure a superior appearance. Ditto paper and copies from similar quality reproducing machines are not recommended for producing an outstanding resume.

Paper size most recommended is 8½″ x 11″. Using a different size is permitted when good taste and readability are maintained.

Stationery stores do not always stock the desired color, texture, and weight of paper preferred; in this case, contact a paper distributor in your area.

C. Type style

Choose an easy-to-read type style; avoid ornate, decorative, or Old English type styles.

D. Reproduction

If you cannot type each resume individually, a most impressive method of printing your resume is to have it varityped and reproduced by a professional printer. Varityping allows you to place emphasis by the use of more than one size of letters, type style, and level of darkness on the same page. "Printers" are listed in the Yellow Pages of your telephone directory. The charge for 100 copies of a one-page, varityped resume, on 35 lb. linen paper will be approximately $13.

Resume Format: Examples

Your next decision will be to select a format which will best convey your qualifications to the employer. The following three formats are offered to stimulate your thinking: categorical format, achievement format, and letter format.

A. Categorical format

In this approach, your qualifications are grouped into easily recognized categories such as: education, work experience, extracurricular activities, summer jobs, military experience, and so on. Place the category with your most impressive qualifications first. Proceed to list categories in order of decreasing importance. Be sure that each category is presented in light of the employer's job description and selection criteria.

The examples in this section are included to illustrate attempts at devising an outstanding resume which would serve as an effective sales presentation. You will notice that each has tried to define his or her job objective as clearly as possible and to emphasize the strongest qualifications for the desired job. Each candidate has decided that education is his or her strongest qualification for the job objective.

We have purposely selected a group of candidates who have the same degree: master of business administration. Each candidate completed identical course work, except for elective courses; however, you will notice great differences in the presentation of the degree and its content. Specific courses and special studies were emphasized to illustrate the candidate's qualifications for the job objective as stated. Observe the differences as you read the examples.

A similar approach should be used in relating your work experience, extracurricular activities, and so on to the job objective.

Each resume example is preceded by employer data including: job title, duties, and desired qualifications. Notice that each resume is focused upon the employer data.

Employer data

Job title: Marketing manager.
Duties: Design and implement a complete marketing program for a new line of transistorized components. Responsibilities will include the definition of both domestic and international markets and development of U.S. government market.
Qualifications: Master's degree in business administration with an emphasis in marketing. Familiarity with sophisticated techniques of marketing research and product distribution. Minimum of five years' experience in proposals and contract negotiations for U.S. government funded projects.

Peter Phifer
1223 Pickled Pepper Place
Los Angeles, California 93330
(213) 654-7654

job
objective

A position as MARKETING MANAGER for a technologically-oriented manufacturing organization. Responsibilities desired include the design and implementation of a marketing program for a new product line.

education

UNIVERSITY OF SOUTHERN CALIFORNIA
Candidate for Master of Business Administration degree in June 19—. Emphasis in Marketing with course work including: research methods in marketing, international marketing, marketing models, and industrial and governmental marketing. Additional courses and research studies covered the concepts of marketing channels, institutional structure, comparative retail-wholesale systems, transportation services, inventory management, warehousing, physical distribution systems analysis and planning.

BAYLOR UNIVERSITY
B.S. Electrical Engineering

work
experience

DOMEALTH DEVELOPMENT CORPORATION
SAN FRANCISCO, CALIFORNIA
19— - Present: Senior Systems Analyst
19— - 19—:   Systems Analyst
19— - 19—:   Intelligence Analyst
Senior Systems Analyst: Project planning and contract performance responsibilities on varied R&D project for the federal office of Civil Defense. Responsibilities include proposal writing, presenting project results and ideas for future work to our Pentagon customers, designing approaches to new projects, developing work plans, technical writing, and field work.
Systems Analyst: Involved in a variety of projects for the Federal Office of Civil Defense which resulted in extensive field work with state and local government officials. Significant accomplishments include:
Developed a computer simulation model for radioactive fallout prediction.
Wrote the textbook for a nationwide local government training program currently being conducted by university extension departments in 50 state universities; conducted portions of the first training class for these instructors.
Developed emergency information system for federal regional centers. This project involved defining information requirements, specifying information processing procedures, preparing training manuals, and training federal employees in the use of the system.
Developed an integrated weapons effects reporting system to be used at all levels of government. This system development task

involved the full range of activities as indicated immediately above.

Intelligence Analyst: Member of a two-man unit which supplied all military intelligence information for the corporation. This involved maintaining current threat estimates, frequent intelligence briefings, and preparing summary documentation. Wrote a Vietnam war scenario that is still being used in Air Force training exercises.

| military | A3; no active commitment |
| references | Available upon request |

Employer data

Job title: Salesman.

Duties: Market a line of electronic copiers and office machines. Initial assignment will include a six-month sales training program.

Qualifications: Master's degree in Business Administration with an emphasis in marketing is preferred, no experience necessary, must be a leader type, enjoy working with people, excellent communication skills, high energy, capable of understanding the technical aspects of E.D.P. equipment.

Cecilia Brock
1224 Window Street
Fullerton, California 90191
(714) 749-2652

| job objective | To procure a position as a MARKETING RESEARCH ANALYST or SALES PERSON with a large, technologically oriented corporation in the nondefense electronics industry. |

education   UNIVERSITY OF SOUTHERN CALIFORNIA
Candidate for the degree of Master in Business Administration in June 197-. Electives emphasize marketing strategy, operations management and organizational behavior. An extensive research study was conducted into planning and coordinating research, research methodology, and the analysis, use and evaluation of quantitative models of marketing research.

BONNER COLLEGE, BLOOMINGTON, CALIFORNIA
Received Bachelor of Arts degree, Magna Cum Laude, in Physics in June 196-. Honors and activities include Honors Program, Physics Laboratory Intern, Freshman Physics Award, Spence Science Award, Physics Club, and German Club.

honors and activities   Twice included on Dean's List of Scholastic Excellence. Member and officer of the following organizations: USC Communications Board, Budget Subcommittee Chairman; Daily Trojan Newspaper, Advertising Manager, Sports Writer, Journalist; USC Band, Staff Member, Award of Merit; Alpha Kappa Psi Business Fraternity, Policy Chairman; Association of Students and Business; USC Sailing Club, Publicity Chairman; Alpha Chi, Pledge Class and Chapter Social Chairman; Chancellor's Special Committee on Public Relations.

early background and interests
Grew up in Oregon and Michigan and attended public schools. Active in school government and extracurricular activities. Interests include tennis, auto design, traveling, music and the theatre. Spent summer of 19— traveling in Europe.

references
Personal references available upon request.

Employer data

Job title: Corporate planning analyst.

Duties: Work with a team of analysts in defining avenues of corporate expansion. Evaluate the costs and profitability of proposed ventures and acquisitions within petroleum industry.

Qualifications: Master's Degree in Business Administration with an emphasis in finance. Minimum of three years' experience in manufacturing.

Bee Loving
7200 Forward Lane
Los Angeles, California 90291
(213) 845-8765

job objective
A position on an INTERNAL CONSULTING TEAM with a large corporation in the oil or chemical industry. Procedures of greatest interest include the study of mergers and acquisitions, strategic long-range planning, and operating strategy.

education
UNIVERSITY OF SOUTHERN CALIFORNIA
Candidate for degree of Master in Business Administration, June 19—. Courses include corporate financial management; financial accounting; long-range corporate planning; manufacturing policy; and economic environmental analysis. Research study conducted into analysis of the factors underlying manufacturing costing, theories of interest, capital formation, and economic development.

POLYTECHNIC INSTITUTE OF CALIFORNIA
Received Bachelor of Science in Chemical Engineering degree, June 19—. Managing Editor of ChemEScope; Assistant Editor of Counterweight; Chairman of a Student Symposium of AIChE; member of AIChE.

work experience
UNION OIL COMPANY, June 19— – April 19—
Staff Chemical Engineer. Involved in process and product quality control. Developed spectophotometric analytical method resulting in annual savings of $62,000. As Assistant Personnel Manager, job responsibilities included wage surveys, management training, major project planning and supervision of a new facility costing $73,000 and direct supervision of seven employees.

LEROY LEAD COMPANY, June 19—– August 19—

Assistant to Vice President. Involved in plant relocating feasibility studies, new venture analysis including financial analysis in the area of mergers and acquisitions. Considerable contact with the investment banking community in evaluation of prospective acquisitions.

summer work | RIP VAN WINKLE MATTRESS CO., June 19—– August 19—

Employed as Summer Shutdown Coordinator. Responsibilities included planning, scheduling and implementing a major equipment overhaul program costing approximately $250,000. In addition, supervised projects and vacation relief as machine shop supervisor.

military | UNITED STATES ARMY

On active duty April 19— to April 19— Assigned Ballistics Research Laboratories. Conducted research program in Controlled Cooling of High Explosives. Selected Soldier of Year 19—; Awarded Special Commendation Certificate, Test & Evaluation Command.

personal background | Raised in Los Angeles area. Attended public high school. Activities and interests include Junior Achievement, Industrial Relations Club, Boy Scouts Fund Drive. Spent summer of 19— and fall of 19— traveling in Europe.

references | Personal references available on request.

B. Achievement format

The achievement format may be most effective if you are seeking a position within a field in which you have extensive experience. This approach will best display what the employer wants to see—the *results* of your previous efforts. In using this format, you are not bounded by dates or sequences of experience in bringing your most relevant accomplishments together for emphasis:

a. First, list achievements and results of your efforts which are directly related to the position you are seeking. Start with your most impressive relevant achievement; disregard chronological sequences. You may mix and reorder achievements regardless of **when** they were completed.

b. Second, offer an agenda of employers and job titles. Provide information about your job assignment in this section.

c. Next, offer a listing of educational background with dates and degrees earned.

d. Other information about background and references should complete the resume.

See the following examples.

Employer data

Job: Financial administrator.

Duties: Take charge of financial structuring operations and manage financial activities with greatest efficiency. Responsibilities will include all phases of financial planning and control.

Qualifications: Must be familiar with financial controls and cash management. Knowledgable about public offerings and presenting them for greatest company benefit. Adept at long-range corporate planning.

> Scrooge Tightfist
> 3221 Control Circle
> Pandamonia, Texas 91342
> (512) 862-4231

job objective	A position as FINANCIAL ADMINISTRATOR/BUSINESS PLANNER for a growing public company positioned in the consumer products industry.
achievements	Brought a $4 million contract under control by innovative financial structuring within a period of four months. As controller and treasurer of a manufacturing oriented company in the Southwest, developed a system of controls and cash management which resulted in a 10 percent increase in yearly profits. Restructured a company stock offering to increase net useable capital by 12 percent.
work experience	TURTLESHELLS RESTAURANTS, 19— to 19— *Director of Business Planning:* Responsible for preparing forecasts (operating statistics, profit and loss statements and funds flow statements). Evaluation of revenues and expenses for the purpose of reversing a deteriorating profit situation. Evaluation of corporate financial structuring.
	CARNUBA CARWAX COMPANY, 19— to 19— *Controller and Treasurer:* Responsible for development of new budgeting, forecasting and performance reporting systems. Worked closely with senior management in developing the first formal consolidated annual budget, monthly management report and weekly performance analysis of key indicators. *Financial Analyst:* Responsibilities included reporting monthly performance results to the Board of Directors and senior management including revenue, expense, operating results and industry comparisons. *Budget Analyst:* Responsibilities included coordinating budgeting procedures in four regions (headquartered in Chicago, St. Louis, Los Angeles and Hong Kong), developing and monitoring detailed, computerized expense budgets on a monthly, quarterly and annual basis.
education	NEW YORK UNIVERSITY, 19— to 19— M.B.A. Elected to National Business Honorary, Beta Gamma Sigma.

M.S. Systems Management. Thesis "An Analysis of the Internal Function of Planning."

BALDUS UNIVERSITY, 19— to 19—

B.S., Major Biology, Minor English.

references Available upon request.

Employer data

Job: Plant manager.

Duties: Will be required to lower overhead costs, increase plant efficiency and reliability, and refine production process.

Qualifications: Candidate will have considerable industrial engineering background with good analytic skills to match management abilities. Most importantly—must understand profit and loss relationship to costs.

Hearty Soul
429 Nose-to-the-Grindstone St.
Fresno, California 91236
(209) 727-5627

job objective A position as PLANT MANAGER or INDUSTRIAL ENGINEER with an electronics components manufacturer.

achievements Reduced raw materials purchasing costs 8 percent.
Redesigned plant layout, saving 450 man-hours yearly.
Designed ordering system, saving 250 man-hours and $150,-000 annually.
Developed rapid procurement procedure to expedite parts distribution, reduced average delay from one week to one day.
Converted inventory records from manual to EDP system, increasing reliability and savings of $250,000 annually.

work experience CASH REGISTER MANUFACTURER, 19— to 19—
Senior Industrial Engineer. Responsible for improving efficiency of plant operations and cost reduction. Used EDP systems analysis approach toward evaluating purchasing and inventory record keeping procedures.

NORTHEASTERN MUTUAL LIFE INSURANCE, 19— to 19—
Salesman. Sell life insurance policies to prospective clients by making personal presentations and mail solicitations.

DAN D. DETERGENTS, 19— to 19—
Plant Engineer. Conduct plant time and motion studies to determine techniques of lowering overhead and increasing efficiency.

education B.S. INDUSTRIAL ENGINEERING, COTILLION COLLEGE, 19—
Participated on a work study program to finance education; worked approximately 20 hours each week.

Member of engineering honorary fraternities: Tau Beta Pi and Alpha Pi Mu.

references   References available upon request.

Employer data

Job title: Marketing manager.

Duties: Develop new markets for a line of industrial products and services. Responsibilities will include all marketing strategy and customer definition for company expansion into western United States.

Qualifications: The prime candidate must have a successful marketing background especially in start-up efforts. Must be self-directing, possess good management skills, and be knowledgable about sales, distribution and profits.

Will Gotowork
8721 Eager Street
Petersburg, California 91261
(213) 821-9734

job objective   A position as MARKETING MANAGER for an industrial products distributor or manufacturer with interests in the West.

achievements   Developed markets in the West from zero to $495,000 sales in two years.
Established six product distribution centers with warehouse facilities which became profit-making within one year.
Conceived and successfully sold three new product ideas which increased company sales $100,000 nationwide.
Managed three other salesmen in the West, all of whom met their sales quota every year.

work experience   QUARTOR CONTROLS COMPANY
Marketing Representative, 19— to 19—
Responsible for developing markets in western United States and establishing product distribution centers.
Salesman, 19— to 19—
Responsible for servicing existing accounts and for developing new business by making cold calls. Area included the city of Chicago.

COOK COUNTY, ILLINOIS, 19— to 19—
Manager, Section Team
Responsible for supervising the construction of a portion of state highway. Managed a team of six workers, work scheduling, and inspection.

education   UNIVERSITY OF ILLINOIS, 19— to 19—
Bachelor of Science, Civil Engineering.

| military | LIEUTENANT, Supply Corps, U.S. Navy, 19— to 19— Served as Supply Department Head with direct responsibilities for supervision and training of 45 men. |
| references | References available upon request. |

C. Letter format

This format will be especially valuable when sending unsolicited mailings to companies and when responding to job advertisements.

The sole purpose of this format is to make the reader want to interview you. Offer sufficient relevant information to titillate the reader, to motivate the reader to call you.

Compose the letter in four sections:

1. Attention. Gain the reader's attention by announcing one of your major accomplishments which will be relevant to the company's operations or to the information given in the job advertisement.

2. Interest. Point out that this letter will be of interest to the reader by stating the reason for the letter (e.g., response to newspaper advertisement) or by establishing a match between your skills and the company's activities.

3. Desire. Develop a desire in the reader to meet you by offering a series of examples of your achievements which are relevant to the job. State the *results* or *achievements* of your efforts; do not list your responsibilities or activities.

Offer information about your educational qualifications if they are considered relevant.

4. Action. Guide the reader to action by suggesting a meeting and offering information about reaching you by telephone and by mail.

See the following examples.

Newspaper advertisement

MARKETING VICE PRESIDENT

Exceptional opportunity for a creative individual who possesses high level management and organization skills. This individual will report directly to the president and be instrumental in the conception and start up of the corporate advertising campaign.

A strong marketing management work history connected with the development and implementation of a consumer product sales program is mandatory. Direct mail merchandise experience very desirable. Los Angeles based firm.

Send resume with complete salary history to:

BIMBO BOBO CO.
Subsidiary of INCO. Corp.
4000 Wilshire Blvd., Los Angeles, Calif. 90045

BIMBO BOBO CO.
4000 Wilshire Blvd.
Los Angeles, California 90045

I'm not a conventional person; innovation and creativity are my trademarks.

I've been responsible for start-up operations before. In fact, my current position was a start-up assignment. The results of my work:

Conceived and managed our current marketing operation which has surpassed all competition in design and effectiveness.

Designed and managed a direct-mail advertising promotional program which has resulted in a 400% *increase* in prospects.

Compiled a management information system which has reduced overhead and has enabled an efficient marketing research effort.

As recognition of achievement, I've been appointed Chairman of the Professional Services Committee of an association whose membership is involved in my field.

I've been asked to be program chairman for an annual conference of professionals in my field within the western United States.

Founded and manage a professional society with membership from industry, government, and academic organizations.

Competent in the stimulus/response, A.I.D.A., and the need/satisfaction theories of selling.

I graduated from the USC Graduate School of Business (MBA, Marketing) and School of Engineering (BSEE).

If you are looking for a young, dynamic executive who will settle for nothing less than success, who is hard working, honest—let's talk!

I may be reached by calling (213) 826-2626.

Sincerely,

Newspaper advertisement

GENERAL MANAGER

Multi-plant division of a machinery manufacturer has position for a seasoned professional manager with total profit and loss responsibility.

Prior experience should demonstrate success as a leader at the superintendent or general manager level. This individual will have technical competence in materials management and engineering. This position offers tremendous opportunity for an achiever to see the results of complex planning, organizing and sound decision making.

Ideal southern location, with compensation at a rate established by a progressive corporation which recognizes results.

Send your resume in confidence including salary history and requirements.

Box 120E, The Wall Street Journal, L.A.
Equal Opportunity Employer

The Wall Street Journal
Box 120 E
Los Angeles, California 92121

Gentlemen:

Company profits have grown for four consecutive years since I've held the position as General Manager. My assignment has included total profit and loss responsibilities for a multi-plant manufacturer.

Your advertisement in the *San Francisco Chronicle* outlines the need for a person with my background and qualifications.

The results of my recent assignments have been these:

Managed six plants employing over 3,500 employees and showed a 17 percent increase in profits during my first two years.

Successfully dealt with labor relations problems to keep employees from unionization.

Lowered production costs 12 percent through usage of a comprehensive internal audit program.

Reduced overhead costs by automating materials handling procedures.

I am a graduate of UCLA (MBA, 1969) and Georgia Tech (BS Engineering, 1962).

If your organization is interested in a proven manager, I may be reached by calling (213) 828-2822.

Sincerely,

D. Letter to be sent after an interview

Purpose: To keep your name and qualifications in the mind of the prospective employer.

Destination: Interviewer.

Time: In general, five days after the interview.

Content: Three major topics:

a. Confirm your interest in the available position.

b. Point out a definite match between your qualifications and the employer's needs.

c. Express a willingness for further consideration.

Mr. John Smith, V.P.
General Products
1173 Alegation Street
Porterville, New Jersey

Dear Mr. Smith:

I certainly enjoyed the opportunity to meet with you to discuss the present opening in your organization for a Product Manager. After reflecting upon the information you had provided about the opening, the organization, and the qualifications of the man wanted to fill the position, I feel that the job is the one I am seeking.

I say this because:

A masters degree in business and a bachelors degree in engineering provide an ideal educational background for the position as Product Manager in a small electronics firm.

Two years of experience as a marketing representative with IBM and one year of experience as a staff engineer with Controlled Data Company have exposed me to excellent training in the electronics and data processing market.

The people who have been successful in this position with your organization have similar personal data, educational background, and experience to mine.

The promotional system used in your organization and earnings potential are in accord with what I am seeking.

I hope to be seriously considered as an employee; I will be pleased to discuss my qualifications in further detail at your convenience. Thank you.

Very truly yours,

Mr. Anon Ymous
Specific Tings Co.
8143 Bones Boulevard
Los Angeles, California

Dear Mr. Ymous:

Thank you for taking the time to discuss your company and the recent opening, Assistant Controller, with me. I have been giving careful thought and consideration to the facts presented at our meeting concerning the company's present needs. Taking my present abilities and future plans into account, I feel we have a match.

The task as we discussed it is a three-step process: problem definition, solution design, and solution implementation. My CPA certificate and accounting experience combined with my M.B.A. degree provide me with the necessary blend of the specialist's abilities with the generalist's perspective to do the job.

After our meeting, I met with one of the men working in the department now; his ideas and comments, along with the information you provided about the direction and future goals of the organization, helped me in gaining a better understanding of the company's makeup.

My thanks again for your time. I certainly would be interested in exploring the position with your organization; please call upon me to offer additional information.

Sincerely,

150

E. Tailored format

In this approach, your skills and resources are presented in a manner which shows their fit with the specific job in question.

This approach may be most suitable for applicants who have a marginal amount of formal education. Lack of formal education may not be a liability if you can show other facts which indicate that you are capable of doing the job *as desired by the employer*.

No resume writing technique can get you a job for which you do not qualify. If you are convinced that you *are* qualified for the position, the task ahead is to write out the reasoning process you used to arrive at that conclusion . . . in the form of a resume. Your work experience will most likely be the source of your qualifications; the challenge will be to interpret your experience in the form of skills and to show relevance between your skills and the employer's requirements. Some of the following resume examples will demonstrate the concept.

Write your resume in one of two ways:

Tailored Format A.

List the selection criteria which will be used by the employer; then display your qualifications to show their applicability to each of the criteria.

Tailored Format B.

List the functional responsibilities of the job; then display your qualifications to show their applicability to each responsibility.

Your decision to select Format A or Format B will be determined by the availability of job and employer information.

Let's review a few examples to illustrate the concept. We have selected applicants whose formal education is not directly relevant to the job in question; in most cases, work experience was also not directly relevant.

Read the following job description for a distribution relations manager.

Job title:	Distribution Relations Manager—West Coast
Duties:	Establish and maintain relations with the retail distributors of our line of zippers and sewing supplies. Conduct in-store sewing demonstrations for customers to stimulate sales. Assist department buyers in ordering and display of our products.
Qualifications:	Experience in oral presentations and demonstrations, familiar with business activities and the profit motive. Must be willing to travel. Skill in sewing desirable.
Contact:	Clark Kent Super Zippers Co. 1401 Main Street Minneapolis, Minnesota 49027

Assume for a moment that you are Clark Kent, the employer. The resume of Joan Moran, shown in the accompanying illustration, has been put on your desk.

Last Name	First Name	Middle Maiden, and/or previous name		Areas of Specialization		Date 9/12/--
MORAN	JOAN	SIMPSON		1. Secondary Ed.	2. N/A	

Street Address___16 Bellvue Circle___

City and State___Saint Paul, Minn.   49027___
(zip)

Current Job Title___Teacher___

Date of Birth__11-14-44__   Sex__F__
mo.-day-year

Height__5'4"__   Weight__125__

Telephone__(613) 794-3991__   Social Security Number__570-45-6363__

Military Status__N/A__

Marital Status__Married__

EDUCATIONAL BACKGROUND

Degree:	Institution	Major	Minor	Date Completed or Expected Completion
Bachelors	University of Minnesota	English	Communications/ Social Studies	19--
Masters	N/A			
Doctorate	N/A			

Thesis or Dissertation Title: "Literature as a Social Indicator"

PROFESSIONAL BACKGROUND

Credentials Held or Applied for | Secondary Teaching Credential, State of Minnesota

Years of Teaching Experience	Elem.	Sec.	J.C.	Col.	Univ.	Total
		6				6

SPECIAL INFORMATION

OPTIONAL   Served as Chairperson of English Dept.,
Faculty representative to District Teacher's Association,
Advisor to Debate and Speech Club

—EMPLOYMENT HISTORY—

LAST OR PRESENT EMPLOYER

NAME___Saint Paul School District___

From 19____
To   19____   Position Title:___Teacher___   Part Time____
Full Time___X

District or Institution:___Lakeview School___

Name and Title of Supervisor:___Mr. John Simpson___

Duties:___Teach English and Social Studies to 11th and 12th grades___

NEXT PREVIOUS

From 19____
To   19____   Position Title:___N/A___   Part Time____
Full Time____

District or Institution:___

Name and Title of Supervisor:___

Duties:___

NEXT PREVIOUS

From 19____
To   19____   Position Title:___N/A___   Part Time____
Full Time____

District or Institution:___

Name and Title of Supervisor:___

Duties:___

After reading about Joan Moran, are you strongly disposed to wanting to meet her? Is she well qualified for the job? Are you impressed that she could definitely do the required job?

152

May I assume that your response to each of the above questions is "NO?"

We've rewritten Joan Moran's resume using Format A and then again using Format B. You are still Clark Kent; please read these two new renditions of Joan's qualifications:

Format A

Joan Moran
16 Bellvue Circle
Saint Paul, Minnesota   49027

(613) 794-3991 (day)   (613) 465-3145 (evening)

job objective	A position in the retailing industry with a retailer or manufacturer. Responsibilities desired include product promotion/customer service.
selection criteria and corresponding qualifications	**A. EXPERIENCE IN ORAL PRESENTATIONS AND DEMONSTRATIONS**

    1. Skill in effective oral presentations has been developed by six years of teaching on the secondary level; presentations were prepared and delivered daily; extemporaneous presentations were offered regularly.

    2. Formal and informal presentations and discussion group sessions were conducted for PTA and other community adult groups.

    3. Training sessions were designed and conducted for in-service day programs which were attended by adult women.

    4. Featured as guest speaker at student interest clubs and off-campus student programs.

B. FAMILIARITY WITH RETAILING AND BUSINESS

    1. Experience as retail sales clerk and stock clerk during summers and vacations while attending college.

    2. Participated in a store-wide inventory at year's end; as a result became aware of item coding, data storage and retrieval, and the use of sales data in future ordering.

C. WILLING TO TRAVEL

    1. Two grown children and a spouse who travels frequently make up a personal family situation which will allow a position requiring frequent travel.

Format A (continued)

  2. Familiar with the travel situation because of having conducted regular summer tours (3-week programs) for student groups during summer vacations.

 D. SKILLS IN SEWING

  1. Sewing has been a hobby for 15 years; experience has been focused upon teenage and adult women's fashions.

  2. Completed a "beginning sewing" course offered through the adult education program in our area.

work experience Secondary Teacher   Saint Paul School District
                19___ to 19___

Responsibilities included teaching assignments in English and social studies. Elected faculty representative to the District Teacher Association and appointed advisor to the student debate squad and speech club. Served as chairperson of the English Dept.

education Bachelor of Arts   University of Minnesota, 19___
      Major: English
      Minor: Communications, Social Studies

References available upon request.

Format B

Joan Moran
16 Bellvue Circle
Saint Paul, Minnesota 49027

(613) 794-3991 (day) (613) 465-3145 (evening)

job objective A position in the retailing industry with a retailer or manufacturer. Responsibilities desired include product promotion/customer service.

functional responsibilities and corresponding qualifications A. ESTABLISH AND MAINTAIN RELATIONS WITH THE RETAIL DISTRIBUTORS OF THE COMPANY LINE OF ZIPPERS AND SEWING SUPPLIES.

  My ability to meet and establish an ongoing relationship with people has been developed through responsibilities like the following:

Format B (continued)

1. As school representative for the District Teacher's Association, I attended monthly conferences, led discussions with special interest groups, and offered presentations.
2. Conducted meetings within the school to discuss teacher needs enabling me to act as their representative to Teacher Associations.
3. Initiated and conducted meetings within the district for special projects.
4. Elected chairperson of the English Department, where my responsibilities included getting to know the department members and their concerns, facilitating problems between department members, and establishing a series of workshops.
5. Parent/Teacher Conferences are conducted four times each year. As I met with the parents of each student, I had to gain their respect and build confidence in a few short minutes, convey to them an evaluation of their child's academic performance (a very emotional topic), and gain their cooperation in implementing the necessary steps for improvement. This experience has prepared me to maintain any one-to-one interface relationship!

B. CONDUCT IN-STORE DEMONSTRATIONS TO STIMULATE SALES.

1. As a result of six years of classroom presentations with varied groups, I've developed the ability to be sensitive to the needs and interests of each group; with that sensitivity, communication with the group is achieved more often than not.
2. Responsibilities as advisor to the debate squad and speech club have helped to develop skills in the compilation of formal presentations, delivery of presentations, and use of audience reviews in presentation improvement.

C. ASSIST DEPARTMENT BUYERS IN ORDERING.

1. Acquainted with the use of information systems and their use as a result of experience in course catalog preparation.
2. Member of a committee designed to research report card systems and their value.

work experience	Secondary Teacher	Saint Paul School District 19___ to 19___

Responsibilities included teaching assignments in English and social studies. Elected faculty representative to the District Teacher's Association and appointed advisor to the student debate squad and speech club.

education	Bachelor of Arts	University of Minnesota, 19___

Major: English
Minor: Communications, Social Studies

References available upon request.

Now, after reading about the "new" Joan, are you strongly disposed to wanting to meet her? Does she seem qualified? Do you have the impression that she could do the job?

May I assume that your response is "Yes?" If so, I agree with you.

In this example, Joan could have used either of the formats to depict her qualifications for the job because the job description provided good, useful information about the functional responsibilities and about the selection criteria to be used. Oftentimes, a job description offers useful information about the functional responsibilities of the job but the selection criteria are missing or too general to be used in compiling a resume; that is the case in the next example.

Job title: Marketing Research Analyst

Duties: Conduct a variety of marketing research projects to provide the necessary information in lauching an effective sales program. Company manufactures and distributes recreational vehicles, camping equipment, and other family recreational items.

Contact: Lyndon Reagan
Recreation Products Inc.
1401 Starlight Ave.
Kansas City, Kansas   09131

Notice the lack of useful information about the selection criteria to be used. The applicant must use Format B (functional responsibilities). As in the previous example, please assume the identity of the employer; you are now Lyndon Reagan. Bolde Ruler's resume has been put on your desk.

Bolde Ruler
182 Secretariat Lane
Louisville, Kentucky   43190
(612) 746-2425

<table>
<tr><td>

job
objective

</td><td>

A position with a consumer goods manufacturer. Desired responsibilities include research projects and data gathering.

</td></tr>
<tr><td>

competencies
in research

</td><td>

A. SKILLS IN SECONDARY RESEARCH

</td></tr>
</table>

A plentiful supply of secondary information is often available to satisfy the researcher's needs. This data is available immediately and at little or no cost. My skills in this area are outlined below:

1. Fully competent in the use of the library resources in our country. Completed two formal college courses in library design and usage, used library resources constantly in the preparation of papers and research projects while enrolled in college and in my current profession, familiar with computer-based data storage and retrieval systems used in libraries.

2. Knowledgeable about the plethora of published data available through federal and state governments. Three useful summaries I've found to be most helpful:

   a. The *Statistical Abstract of the United States,* issued each year, lists more than 1,000 works being published by the federal government and other groups. References to world markets are included. It also contains a "Bibliography of Sources and Statistics" that lists all *Abstract* sources, classified by type of subject. It is probably the best starting point for locating statistical data.

   b. The *County and City Data Book* gives more local, geographical detail than the *Abstract.* It presents a selection of statistics for all counties and cities with a population of more than 25,000.

   c. *Survey of Current Business* features current data on a wide variety of subjects along with statistics and economic trend data.

3. Competent in identifying and using private research organizations, advertising agencies, newspapers, and magazines to gather published data.

4. Aware of and competent in locating research data made available by subscription to research firms and through membership in trade associations.

     B.   SKILLS IN PRIMARY RESEARCH

Because of its higher cost, primary data is used only when secondary information is not meeting the need. I am acquainted with and have experience in the following types of primary research:

1. Observation method—avoidance of direct questioning.
2. Survey method—telephone, mail, and interviewing techniques.
3. Experimental method—a combination of the two methods above with the establishment of control groups and the application of statistical analysis.

     C.   SKILLS IN PROBLEM SOLVING

Recognizing the value in using a scientific approach to solving marketing research problems, I wish to reaffirm my grasp of the four stage approach to problem solving (retrieved from my education in logic):

1. Definition of the problem.
2. Analysis of the situation.
3. Informal investigation.
4. Formal research.

work experience Louisville Welfare Program   Oct. 19__ to 19__
Louisville, Kentucky

Responsibilities as social worker included meeting with clients, developing recommendations for rehabilitation program, administration of welfare funds, and compiling annual trend reports on city welfare program.

education Kentucky Community College
                                          June 19__
Major—Education   Minor—Library Science
Developed skills in the uses and design of library resources.

References available upon request.

Let's take another example. In the job description for management trainee, you'll notice more useful data in the section on selection criteria.

Job title:	Management Trainee
Duties:	Formal comprehensive training program for individuals to over-see the operation of a family restaurant. Gain administrative experience in quality control and public relations. Good start-ing salary and regular reviews based on initiative and respon-sible performance.
Qualifications:	Formal education in the basics of business and the concepts re-lated to management, finance, and marketing. Must have had experience in an administrative capacity and competent in managing several responsibilities at the same time.
Contact:	Pepper Oné Crusty Pizza Parlor 81 Pompadora Rd. Crust, Texas 24105

You are now Pepper Oné; Georgia Doser's resume has been put before you.

Georgia Doser
2642 Lighthouse Lane
Houston, Texas   24106

(314) 792–4221 (day)   (314) 911–3141 (evening)

job
objective

A position in the food service industry with a company which offers training in the management and operation of a restaurant facility.

selection
criteria
and
corresponding
qualifications

A. FORMAL EDUCATION IN THE BASICS OF BUSINESS AND MANAGEMENT

Formal education has included a review of mana-gerial processes with emphasis upon organizational behavior, authority/responsibility relationships, work projects design and delegation, and time/performance coordination. Course work related to marketing processes included concepts of com-munication and persuasion in written and oral formats.

The above were part of the curriculum as I com-pleted the qualifications for an Associate of Arts de-gree in administration at the Texas Business School, June 19___.

B. EXPERIENCE IN AN ADMINISTRATIVE CAPACITY

Administrative skills have been developed through participation in volunteer programs, administration, and avocational pursuits as the following examples will illustrate:

1. In our neighborhood elementary school, acted as a grade level representative and as program coordinator where responsibilities included the administration of faculty and parent programs, scheduling of activities, and monitoring of results.
2. Served as parent assistant to vice principal with responsibilities for student discipline and correction.
3. Managed summer athletic programs in our neighborhood.
4. Acted as vice president of our local home owner's association.
5. Elected and served as chairperson of the Westchester Ladies Club, an organization which is part of our church.

19___ to present

References available upon request.

Summary

Purpose of a resume is to get you invited to interviews. Your resume will serve this purpose if it shows the employer that you are able to satisfy the company's needs.

Necessary preliminary information includes:
   a.   *Your qualifications.*
   b.   *The prospective employer's job description and selection criteria.*

Rank your qualifications according to their ability to complement the employer's selection criteria. Describe each of the areas from the employer's viewpoint.

Consider the following physical aspects of your resume to insure that it will be distinctive, impressive, and professional: length, paper, type style, and reproduction.

Resume formats include: categorical format, achievement format, and letter format.

10 | *How to handle a job interview . . . regardless of the situation*

Interviewers Aren't Gods: You Take Charge

Dispel your idea that all interviewers know what they are doing.

People who conduct interviews are not always knowledgeable about how to interview. Many are inept listeners; others are confusing, unintelligible speakers. Oftentimes, you'll be interviewed by employees from the finance or engineering department who have no training in how to conduct an interview.

Don't let their role as interviewers intimidate you or make you nervous. After reading this chapter, you'll probably know more about interviewing than they.

One of the biggest mistakes made in an interview is embodied in the anxious applicant who is waiting to be asked a question, any question, upon which the flood gates open and a life biography rushes out as if it were a canned oration. The same oration comes out regardless of the company being interviewed or the job being considered.

Another typical mistake is apparent in the applicant quietly waiting for the interviewer to conduct the entire meeting by throwing a sequence of questions. The applicant answers each question quickly and poorly in expectation of the next question.

An experienced, professional, competent interviewer would not allow such mistakes to occur. A good interviewer will draw out the applicant, develop a sense of communication, and then proceed to evaluate the match between the company's needs and the applicant's ability to satisfy those needs. Unfortunately, you'll encounter more inept interviewers than any other kind.

Therefore, *you* should take charge of every interview. If the interviewer is a good one, he'll know what you're doing and it will be exactly what he wants. If the interviewer happens to be a boob, you've protected yourself from his inability.

Place your fate in *your* hands; you conduct the interview. Interviewers aren't gods.

Your preparation for a job interview requires that you are:

Thoroughly familiar with your qualifications.

Knowledgable about the company offering the position.

Assured that your qualifications match those required to perform the job.

Because of the preliminary research you have conducted about yourself and about the company, you should be equipped with the information and raw data needed to offer a convincing presentation about the match between your abilities and the company's needs. The next step is to select the proper presentation, to display yourself in the interview to achieve the desired objective.

Consider the job interview to be a place where you will be selling yourself to the interviewer. The success of the sales presentation will depend upon your ability to communicate with the interviewer—a giving and taking of relevant, meaningful information.

Keep in mind that "communicate" does not merely mean "tell." You want the interviewer to hear what you say but, also, to evaluate the information and to arrive at the favorable conclusion that you are an excellent candidate for the position. For this reason, the need-satisfaction theory of selling will be most applicable to the task of selling yourself to the interviewer.

Need-satisfaction theory of selling

The need-satisfaction theory of selling assumes that purchases are made to satisfy needs. Therefore, in order to make the sale, you must discover the company's needs and show your ability to satisfy those needs. Developing communication in the presentation is a critical aspect of this approach.

Three sequential phases are involved in this approach to job interviewing:

Phase I.   Need development.

Phase II.   Need awareness.

Phase III. Need satisfaction.

Using the approach as outlined will establish the necessary communication between the interviewer and job seeker before launching into an in-depth evaluation of your qualifications.

Phase I. Need development. You will ask questions of the interviewer which elicit conversation on the company's present needs. Each reply should trigger the next question. The goal is to get the interviewer to talk about company needs in the area of interest to you. Using the questions outlined in Chapter 3 will get you started.

In Phase I, the beginning of the interview, lead the interviewer into discussing the company, the department, the job to be done, and the selection criteria to be used for identifying the ideal candidate for the position. Ask questions which force the interviewer to do most of the talking; your goal is to get the interviewer to talk about what is needed. The interviewer is primarily interested in what you can do for the company. Do not ask questions about what the company can do for you such as: pension systems, annual bonuses, hospital benefits, vacations, holidays, travel problems, or about the possibility of your having to move. Use the questions outlined in Chapter 3 for developing Phase I.

Each employer has his own ideas about the type of person and set of skills needed to perform any given job. You will go to the interview fully equipped with a complete presentation of how you can do anything, for any employer, in any situation. The temptation is strong for you to offer this "canned oration" covering your full background and capabilities in each interview. Don't succumb to the temptation.

In the beginning of the interview, refrain from talking about what you can do. Instead, concentrate on discovering the employer's needs or perception of those needs. Later, after those needs have surfaced and are understood, your skills and abilities which satisfy the needs will constitute the basis for your "sales presentation." Do not use all of your background experience, skills, abilities, citations, rewards, and so on in the sales presentation; rather, use only those points which satisfy the needs.

Phase II. Need awareness. You take over more of the conversation in trying to have the interviewer recognize and state the company needs specifically.

In Phase II, your goal will be to identify and agree upon the needs *with the interviewer.* Ask questions which center about the needs you have detected in Phase I. Be sure that you see and understand the needs as the interviewer does.

You may feel that because of the recommended research conducted before the interview, you already know the company's needs and, therefore, there is no point in discussing these points with the interviewer. Untrue!

Allow the interviewer to tell you about the company's needs. When he or she feels that you know about the needs and have gained an understanding of them from the immediate conversation, they are likely to feel that a mutual sense of understanding and communication has been reached. If, on the other hand, you try to jump into the conversation too quickly, presenting yourself as company-wide panacea, the interviewer may build up a resentment. Consequently, developing an understanding of the company's needs *together* is the best approach.

Phase III. Need fulfillment. You do most of the talking to show the interviewer how your present abilities qualify you to satisfy those needs. Call upon work experience, education, and other background to verify the abilities needed.

In Phase III, the interviewer and you agree on the needs of the company. This is the time for you to do most of the talking; describe your qualifications to the interviewer. Concentrate on those aspects of your qualifications which meet the company needs rather than presenting a complete scenario of your background, education, and experience. Highlighting certain specific aspects of your qualifications which meet the needs directly will result in a more impressive and convincing presentation.

You are showing the interviewer how the company needs will be fulfilled by hiring you.

How to Handle Each Interview Situation

You may encounter one or more of the following interview situations while conducting a job search.

Think over *your* approach to each situation.

"The talker."
"The inquisition."
"The salesman."
"Acting dumb."
"The quiet one."
"The recorder."
"Not quite qualified."
"Lower level position."
"Pressed."

"The talker"

Situation: After a brief glance at your resume, the interviewer talks endlessly about the company and its activities within the industry. You are not offered the opportunity to speak.

Common response: Candidate listens attentively until the time allotted for the interview runs out. Leaves frustrated. . . .

Because of time limitations the candidate offers a rushed brief description of background and activities. . . .

Recommended response: View this as a stroke of *good luck!*

Phase I of the need-satisfaction approach to selling is exactly this—i.e., get the interviewer to talk about the company and its activities. Since the interviewer has launched into the presentation, the first step has been started for you.

Listen very carefully while the interviewer speaks. Guide the comments and facts to your area of interest through your questions. Let the talk move *around* as well as *to* the points of most interest to you. Be attuned to the areas of greatest interest; decide which areas of the company are of greatest concern to the interviewer. During this period, be gathering the list of "company needs" to which you will be addressing yourself in Phases II and III. Use the questions outlined in Chapter 3 to develop Phase I.

As soon as you detect the interviewer starting to repeat, now is the time for you to show the interviewer that you've been listening; list a few of the points made. Ask for agreement that you've correctly interpreted what you've heard. Ask if you've missed any important points. Your efforts are to gain a mutual agreement upon the company's needs.

Use Phase III to illustrate your abilities to satisfy the needs. Address yourself to each of the points made in the interviewer's presentation.

"The inquisition"

Situation: The interviewer continues to read and reread your resume and fires a series of probing questions about your motives, background, and results of your experience.

Common response: No rapport is established, candidate continues to answer questions as they come, without knowing the interviewer's line of thought. . . .

The candidate gets nervous and offers poor responses to the questions. . . .

Candidate becomes defensive which causes unfavorable feelings with interviewer. . . .

Recommended response: You may be wondering if you've walked into an "inquisition" instead of an "interview."

Sometimes interviewers do not know how to conduct an interview. They may know the criteria used for selecting the proper candidate; however, they may be unknowledgeable about using the interview to evaluate the candidate. The approach being used is a poor one. Getting to know you will be extremely difficult.

You take charge. Remember that you want to start Phase I of the need-satisfaction approach; get the interviewer to talk. Do so by answering the interviewer's questions with comprehensive statements of facts and examples, and by referring to specific accomplishments. Do not offer a one-word or one-sentence answer to any question. Your task is to engage the interviewer in a discussion; get them away from the inquisition.

As you offer the longer answers, the interviewer will become more relaxed. End your answer with a question which will start Phase I. It may take several tries before Phase I is begun. If after several tries to launch Phase I, the interviewer persists in the inquisition approach, your comprehensive answers and references to specific accomplishments have conveyed your qualifications most impressively under the circumstances. You will have made the best of the situation.

"The salesman"

Situation: The interviewer disregards your resume and launches into a descriptive informative sales talk on the virtues of the company.
Common response: The candidate listens to the presentation by the interviewer enduringly while anticipating a turn to speak. . . .
Candidate leaves uncertain about the purpose for the meeting. . . .
Recommended response: You've hit the jackpot again!

Phase I is already in progress. Listen carefully to the interviewer; list the points being made. Use questions to guide the interviewer's comments to the area of interest to you.

When you detect the interviewer's presentation becoming repetitious, move into Phase II and then Phase III.

The interviewer may be giving this sales talk to determine your interest in his type of organization or to inform you of its makeup to confirm your understanding of its operation. In either case, all is going well; you are in Phase I.

"Acting dumb"

Situation: The interviewer opens his talk with "Well, what can I do for you?" or "What type of position are you looking for?"
Common response: Candidate launches into a lengthy discourse on job being sought.
Candidate asks about what the company can offer. . . .
Recommended response: What luck! Again you have been given the perfect opportunity to use your questions to launch into Phase I.

When the question comes, be prepared with the questions you will need to guide the interviewer into telling you all about the organization and especially about the area of interest to you.

Use learned questions, the kind which show that you know something about the field. For example:

> Mr. Smith, I'm quite interested in the field of banking as a career. Your firm, Union Bank, has exhibited very rapid statewide expansion within the past five years; I believe that I've read about your 26th office being opened just last month. Tell me, Mr. Smith, to what do you attribute such rapid successful growth? Is it because of Union's emphasis upon commercial lending development?

This question shows you've done your homework; you will have impressed the interviewer. Continue asking learned questions as each response is offered.

When the time is right, move into Phase II and then to Phase III.

"The quiet one"

Situation: The interviewer begins with a few short questions. Seemingly nervous and quiet, the interviewer resumes by asking you if you have any questions about the job or the company.

Common response: No rapport is established because of strained interview . . .

No rapport is established because interviewer is ill at ease . . .

Unfavorable feelings result in candidate because of strained interview . . .

Recommended response: This interviewer is inexperienced or inept at conducting an interview, probably nervous and doesn't know what to do next. That's good for you.

Help out; you take charge of the interview. Start with the questions you have prepared to launch Phase I.

For example:

> Mr. Johnson, I understand that your company has responded to our nation's need for additional energy sources by amplifying your engineering research department. Is it nuclear engineering that seems most promising? What are the engineers reviewing as alternative energy sources?

Use each of his responses to trigger the next question. Don't let him ramble! Use your questions to have him focus on the area of interest to you.

You'll soon find yourself ready for Phase II and then Phase III.

"The recorder"

Situation: The interviewer asks you a series of questions as your responses are recorded on a form or note pad.

Common response: Candidate answers questions briefly because response is being recorded. . . .

The responses have little continuity because the questions are varied. . . .

Recommended response: In this case, the interviewer may be terribly inexperienced and needs the security of a pen and pad to help—or is completing a company-required form.

Your first task is to get the paperwork completed or stopped. Don't let the pad or form act as a barrier between you and the interviewer.

If the interviewer is filling out a company form, offer to help in completing it; try to work on it "together." As soon as the form is complete, use your statements and questions to launch into Phase I.

If the interviewer is taking personal notes, ask questions which will launch your meeting into Phase I.

You may encounter an interviewer who refuses to stop taking notes. In this case, offer comprehensive answers with examples and references to specific accomplishments to each question. This approach will insure an opportunity to display your qualifications.

"Not quite qualified"

Situation: You and the interviewer have developed a good rapport; however, you are lacking the exact qualifications being sought. You're told so.

Common response: Candidate asks if there is any other job open. . . . Candidate thanks interviewer and leaves. . . .

Recommended response: Don't give up yet. If you feel that you *are* qualified, try the following approach:

Step 1. Review with the interviewer the selection criteria being used to choose the best candidate for the job. If you fit the criteria, reaffirm the match to the interviewer. If you do not, move to Step 2.

Step 2. Ask about the reason for each criteria being used. If the reasons offered are sound, forget the job; you are not qualified for it. If the reasons offered are not completely sound, further discussion with the interviewer may be warranted. Move to Step 3.

Step 3. Point out your views on the questionable reason. Assuming that your view is accepted, offer Phase II and Phase III in the light of the new circumstance.

"Lower level position"

Situation: The interviewer is very impressed with you and your qualifications; however, he offers a lesser position than the one you are seeking.

Common response: Candidate is riddled with self-doubt. . . .

Candidate considers taking job in the hopes that something may come of it. . . .

Recommended response: Don't take the job!

Without written assurance of when you will be promoted and to what office, you are taking a very high-risk career step. If the move does not work out, you will have lost considerable time and your career will have suffered a setback. Why take such a risk? Opportunities for career advancement exist where risk for setback is almost negligible.

If you feel that you do want to work for the organization, suggest that the employer create a new job to fit your skills and experience. A change in organizational structure may result in a much more attractive position without career risk to you.

Your request for designing a new job, a more responsible position, is a fair one. Point out to the employer that your purpose is to reduce the risk in the venture at no one's expense.

When you make the suggestion, be ready with the description of the new job you have in mind. Do not rely on the employer; because of his closeness to the company, he may be unable to readily see an alternative job description.

"Pressed"

Situation: You have been made an offer from Company A. You are still negotiating for a more desirable position with Company B. Company A is pressing you for a decision.

Common response: Candidate asks for more time to think things over. . . .

Accepts the position even though it is not the one wanted. . . .

Tells the company about considering another offer. . . .

Recommended response: If you need more time to make your decision, ask for it.

Tell Company A that you have incomplete negotiations with another prospective employer; ask for up to two weeks to give them an employment decision.

If the amount of time you have requested is unavailable, inform Company B of your dilemma. Ask for an earlier decision date.

Answers to Tough Interview Questions

The following questions are invariably asked of those applying for choice positions.

Think over *your* answer to each of the questions.

What type of job are you seeking?

What are your career plans?

Why do you think you might like to work for our company?

What other companies do you plan to interview?

Why do you want to leave your present job?

What opportunities for promotion exist with your present employer?

What salary are you making and what do you hope to get on your next job?

What is your opinion of your present boss and co-workers?

What are your greatest strengths?

What are your chief liabilities?

Are you willing to take a few psychological tests before we seriously discuss an offer of employment?

Question: What type of job are you seeking?

Answers often given: A position in management or where I could work into a top management position. . . .
I want to be able to utilize my training and education to best advantage. . . .
Where I could work with people. . . .
A job where I wouldn't have to do the same thing every day. . . .
Recommended response: Interviewers ask this seemingly "casual" question to determine if you have decided upon a job objective. Here, they are interested in your short-range plans; a description of your life career goals is inappropriate as an answer to this question.

The sample answers given above do not answer the question. Instead of offering useful information about a job objective, they work as a flashing red light to point out a confused, ill-prepared individual.

When you are confronted with this question, answer it by relating information about the industry, company-type, and job function you are seeking. See example below:

> I am seeking a position within the electronic data processing industry. My preference is to join a company headquartered in Southern California which has a well-diversified group of products and services aimed toward industrial markets. A position in marketing planning or sales would be ideal.

This answer indicates a well-oriented individual.

Question: What are your career plans?

Answers often given: A position in top management, maybe a vice president position. . . .

I plan to be president of a company. . . .

I want to start my own company, eventually. . . .

I'll just wait to see what the future brings; these days, it doesn't pay to plan too far ahead. . . .

Recommended response: This question is usually used to compare your future plans to those of the company. The interviewer wants to know if you perceive the job in question as a short stopping point on the way to your career goal or as a long-term, integral part of your career development.

Be prepared for this question by knowing your career plans *and* the path you plan to take. Show in a very logical way that the job in question is a carefully planned part of your development.

For example:

> My career plans are centered about the real estate industry. In reading and speaking with employees and listening to industry leaders in the field, it has become clear to me that great opportunity lies in the commercial and industrial real estate properties. Real estate brokerage has interested me especially.
>
> Your firm's reputation and depth of experience in commercial and industrial brokerage is excellent. So, I'm seeking an affiliation with the best.

Question: Why do you think you might like to work for our company?

Answers often given: I've heard you've got a good company here. . . .

They say you treat employees well. . . .

A friend told me about his experiences with you so I thought I'd look into what's available. . . .

Your company has a good reputation. . . .

I've heard that the company has the highest salaries in the industry. . . .

Recommended responses: These answers are useless generalizations which do nothing except point out a shallow thinker and poor decision maker.

When you answer:

a. Show that you know the company.

b. Show that you know yourself and have a definite career plan.

c. Show the match between you and the company.

For example:

> Your company has focused its product line and services to the health care industry. My research has helped me to understand that the health care industry will enjoy rapid growth throughout the coming years.

Since my interests lie in the field of health services administration, I have sought out an employer like yourself who plans to participate in the industry's growth. The position we have been discussing requires the skills I've developed through education and recent experience.

This approach will illustrate the logical decision-making process you have used to select a prospective employer.

Question: What other companies do you plan to interview?

Answers often given: I don't want to limit myself; I'm open to many areas. . . .

The usual large companies like IBM, B.A. Bakeries, Bechtel, and Procter and Gamble. . . .

A couple of companies my family is involved with, but I don't want to work with them. . . .

Recommended responses: This "innocent" question is used to tag the individual who is confused about his or her job objective and career goal; only such a person would interview with a series of completely unrelated companies.

The interviewer will quickly know your sense of direction and preparedness by listening to the list of other companies you are interviewing. If the names on your list are in a related industry, have similar products and services, and have other characteristics in common, convincing the interviewer of your sincerity will be much easier. The interviewer will be favorably impressed with your knowledge and exposure to the company's competitors.

If a good reason exists for your interviewing with companies in unrelated industries, explain and point out the continuity in your pursuits. For example:

> I've been interviewing with companies like B. A. Bakeries, Bechtel Corporation, Procter & Gamble, and Johnson's Services Products, because they all have large inventory control departments. Since my main interest lies in the utilization of electronic data processing equipment and its application to the task of inventory control, I've been interviewing with companies who have need for automated control systems.

Question: Why do you want to leave your present job?

Answers often given: Salary is too low. . . .

Salary increase is difficult to get. . . .

I don't like the people I'm working for. . . .

My current employer hasn't offered me a good opportunity. . . .

I'm dissatisfied with my current assignment. . . .

Recommended responses: Do not use interpersonal or emotional problems as an answer to this question. Do not "slam" your boss, co-workers, or the company in your previous place of employment as a reply to this difficult question. These replies, justified or not, are based upon personal opinion.

Be objective, avoid responses which could be interpreted as shortcomings on your part. Three very good reasons for wanting to change jobs:

a. Higher salary potential.
b. More responsibility and opportunity to perform.
c. Opportunity to learn and to develop personally.

Question: What opportunities for promotion exist with your present employer?

Answers most often given: None, really. . . .

Chances are poor because I don't have the necessary background in the field. . . .

Chances are fair, but it would take a long time and I'm not willing to wait around. . . .

Recommended responses: If your reply reveals that opportunities for promotion are poor, the interviewer will want to know if your personal shortcomings are keeping you back. If so, are those shortcomings detrimental to the firm.

If your reply points out that your chances for promotion are good, the company will be more inclined to think you are a desirable employee.

You may want to answer this question by relating the results of your recent assignments and comparing them to company expectations. Allow the interviewer to make the judgment that, based upon your performance, a promotion was earned.

Question: What salary are you making and what do you hope to get on your next job?

Answers often given: I was making _____, but there was a special reason is was so low. . . .

I'd expect at least the going rate for the position we are discussing. . . .

I'm asking for a large salary increase over my last job because my company paid a low salary traditionally. . . .

I hope to be paid what I'm worth. . . .

Recommended responses: Timing is all important in answering the question about the salary you are seeking.

If the question is put to you early in the interview session, don't answer it. Dodge the issue by saying that you are unable to offer a figure until you have a clear understanding of the job assignment; ask for more time to discuss the position and your qualifications. You will want the interviewer to be "sold" on you before a price is quoted; this may take more than one interview. Once the interviewer is thoroughly familiar with your qualifications and is convinced that you can do the job, your bargaining position will be greatly enhanced.

When asked about your current salary, you may feel ill at ease if your current salary is exceptionally low or if your salary reflects only a portion of your total compensation package. In response to the question, feel free to state your salary with the corresponding explanation, i.e., you are changing jobs because your salary is well below average for the industry—or your salary is only one component of a compensation package which has a yearly total worth of. . . .

Don't go to a job interview before knowing the salary range for the position. A myriad of salary studies are available for your perusal through government agencies and professional societies. Check with a research librarian to uncover sources of salary data. When a prospective employer asks for your salary requirements, quote the information you have about salary ranges and the sources of your information. Next, identify the portion of the range in which you fit (high, middle, or low) and substantiate your request with facts about your qualifications and background.

Question: What is your opinion of your present
boss and co-workers?

Answers often given: The boss was always busy protecting his little empire. . . .
The boss was a slave driver. . . .
The boss didn't really have the operation under control. . . .
Many of the workers were incompetent and lazy. . . .
They didn't appreciate me and my contributions to the company. . . .

Recommended responses: Answer this question objectively; avoid using personal opinion. Try to use statements which refer to the department or project rather than to the individuals involved. Do not give the impression that you are out to slander all who fall into disfavor with you.
Sample answers:

Our manager was responsible for over 30 people and had six different projects to coordinate. It was quite an assignment for anyone.

The people in our area had quite a diversity of backgrounds and skills; coordinating such an array was quite an assignment.

Our project was a challenging assignment; everyone found their responsibilities to be highly demanding.

Question: *What are your greatest strengths?*

Answers often given: I have a good education and I'm a hard
   worker. . . .
   Willingness to learn and to accept responsibility. . . .
   Good rapport with people; they like me. . . .
   Proven ability to get the job done. . . .

Recommended responses: Make your answer useful to the interviewer
   and relevant to the job in question. Concentrate upon your work-
   related strengths and especially those traits and abilities which will
   be required in the job you are discussing with the interviewer.

   Give plenty of examples for each statement you make; if an example
is not available, don't use the statement!

   Use this question as an opportunity to reaffirm the match between
company needs and your abilities. Talk about personal skills and abilities which relate directly to the job in question. Disregard the request
for information about "greatest strengths"; rather, focus upon *relevant
strengths.*

   Give plenty of examples to substantiate each statement you make; if
an example is not available, don't use the statement!

Question: *What are your chief liabilities?*

Answers often given: I can't think of anything right off hand. . . .

Recommended responses: Only a very immature, naive person would
   offer the response above. Be aware of your weaknesses; don't be
   caught off guard with this question.

   As you mention a few of your weaknesses, follow each statement
with what you have done or plan to do to overcome that weakness. A
most impressive picture of a person who has insight, is realistic, and has
the maturity and drive to recognize and deal with his weaknesses will
emerge.

   Do not bring up unsolved weaknesses which are irrelevant to the
discussion.

   For example:

> Since my latest promotion to a managerial function I've noticed an
> increasing demand on my time especially for reading the latest publi-
> cations in my field and in-house company reports. Realizing that my
> reading speed was not up to par, I enrolled in one of those speed
> reading courses. Although I am still working on increasing my speed,
> I've been enjoying definite results from the course. . . . or . . .
>
> As you know, most of my previous experience has been in technical
> engineering and research. I'm just realizing the need to be sensitive to
> behavior problems in managing people within the department. So I en-

rolled in one of the six-day seminars offered by the local university to help me understand organizational management. We've covered the concepts of personal motivation, personal needs, and building trust in your co-workers. The course is really helping me.

Do not bring up unsolved weaknesses which have no relevance to the discussion.

Question: Are you willing to take a few psychological tests before we seriously discuss an offer of employment?

Answers often given: Yes. . . .

No. . . .

What can those tests tell you; what are you trying to find out about me. . . .

Do you sincerely believe that a few hours of testing can fairly evaluate over 16 years of education and years of successful experience. . . .

Recommended responses: Your answer should be yes. The interviewer would not have posed the question unless the tests were the company's policy.

If your answer is no, you may have killed your chances for the job. The interviewer will immediately think that you are trying to hide something—regardless of your lengthy explanation.

Put yourself at ease before the tests by finding out about them. When a date is arranged for you to take the tests, request a session with the testing company or the test administrator a few days in advance. Ask for a complete description of the test content, its purpose, and scoring approach. Knowledge of the process will dispel your nervousness and apprehensiveness.

Details

1. Know the exact time and place of the interview; keep the information on paper and carry it with you.

2. Get the full name of the company and its pronunciation. Know its parent company and other subsidiaries if they exist.

3. Be certain you have the interviewer's full name and its pronunciation.

4. Carry a small notebook and pen in your pocket or purse.

5. Be on time. Late arrival for a job interview is almost inexcusable. Allow time for traffic tieups, parking difficulties, and slow elevators.

6. Attire. Dress in a manner that will center attention upon what you are saying rather than what you are wearing. Select a mode of dress in which you expect the interviewer to be attired. In general, men should wear a suit rather than sports jacket. Women should select a low key,

daytime ensemble; avoid flamboyant colors and evening wear styles.

7. Be clean shaven; wear a conservative style of haircut and side-burns. Beards, "muttonchop" sideburns, or shoulder length hair for men will distract the interviewer's attention and may cause an unfair bias against you. Why take the risk of losing a job offer because of a nar-row-minded or prejudiced interviewer? Remember, hair grows back!

Summary

You take charge of each interview by implementing the need-satisfaction theory of selling.

The theory consists of three phases:
  Phase   I. Need development.
  Phase II. Need awareness.
  Phase III. Need satisfaction.

Apply the three-phase process to the nine major interview situations as they are encountered.

Appendixes

Appendix A

Reference volumes useful in compiling lists of companies and prospective employers

The references listed in Appendix A represent extremely valuable and useful resources in researching career opportunities; they will be found in major libraries. Use them regularly to make lists of prospective companies, contacts, and to gain important information to help you in your efforts. You'll find these references valuable even after you are employed; they'll help you in doing your job better.

Titles are grouped according to industry or profession. References which cover many areas, useful for a multitude of purposes, are listed in the section entitled: "Directories and References."

Advertising
Art
Banking
Communications
Conservation and environment
Consulting
Directories and references
Education and teaching
Electronics
Entertainment
Engineering
Food processing and distributing
Foundations
Government
Health services
Home economists

Hotel and travel
Insurance
International business
Investments
Library and information science
Lists of companies
Manufacturers
Marketing research
Merchandising
Petroleum
Professional associations
Public utilities
Publishing
Public relations
Research centers and laboratories
Social service

Advertising

1. **Standard Directory of Advertisers.** Directory of 17,000 companies that advertise nationally, arranged by industry groupings, with alphabetical index. Gives officers, products, agency, advertising appropriations, media used, etc. Includes a "Trademark Index."
2. **Standard Directory of Advertising Agencies.** National Register Publishing Company. Lists over 4,000 agencies, their key personnel, and accounts handled.
3. **Roster and Organization of the American Association of Advertising Agencies.** AAAA., 8500 Wilshire Boulevard, Beverly Hills, California 90211. Lists member firms alphabetically and by state.

Art

4. **American Art Directory.** New York: R. R. Bowker Company. Museums, art schools, and art associations in the United States; includes lists of art magazines, fellowships, and scholarships, art schools abroad, and other art resources.
5. **Art Direction Buyer's Guide of Art and Photography.** Annual. New York: Art Direction. Lists approximately 2,500 suppliers of art for advertising, illustrations, design, photography, and graphic art services; includes classified listings, representatives, and studio listings, each giving address, telephone number, and services performed.

Banking

6. **Banks of the World.** Fritz Knopp Verlag. Frankfurt am Main.
7. **International Bankers Directory.** Rand McNally.
8. **Moody's Bank and Finance Manual.** Moody's Investors Service, Inc.: Robert Messner. Lists companies alphabetically and also real estate companies.
9. **Operating Banking Offices.** FDIC.
10. **Polk's World Bank Directory.** R. L. Polk & Company, Lists banks and information.
11. **Who's Who in Banking; The Directory of the Banking Profession.** 2d ed. New York: Business Press, Inc.

Communications

12. **Audiovisual Market Place.** Olga S. Weber. 8th ed. R. R. Bowker Company. Company names, addresses, key personnel, and product lines for all active producers, distributors, and other sources of AV learning materials. Includes national, professional, and trade organizations, educational, radio, and TV stations.
13. **Broadcasting Yearbook.** Broadcast publications. List of all TV stations and AM–FM radio stations in United States and Canada, including addresses and telephone numbers, licenses and owner, representatives. Lists names and addresses of radio and TV commercial and program producers, new service distributors, network executives, and research services.

14. **California Publicity Outlets.** Unicorn Systems Company, Information Services Division. Names and addresses of California companies dealing in newspapers and other communication media.
15. **Introduction to Mass Communications.** Edwin Emery, Philip Ault, and Warren Agee. 3d ed. Dodd, Mead and Company.
16. **Organizations, Publications, and Directories in the Mass Media of Communications.** Biennial. Iowa City: School of Journalism, University of Iowa. Lists organizations and their publications, business and professional publications, directories, names and addresses of state press and state broadcasting associations, and other useful information.

Conservation and Environment

17. **Conservation Directory.** Annual. Washington, D.C.: National Wildlife Federation. Lists organizations and agencies concerned with the conservation, management, and use of this country's natural resources.
18. **Directory of Organizations Concerned with Environmental Research.** State University College at Fredonia. Geographic and subject listing of organizations (governmental, university, and private) throughout the world involved in environmental research.
19. **Pollution Control Directory.** Vol. 4, No. 11 of Environmental Science and Technology, American Chemical Society. Lists manufacturers and suppliers of pollution control equipment, products, and services.

Consulting

20. **Consultants and Consulting Organizations.** Paul Wasserman and W. R. Greer, Jr. New York: Graduate School of Business and Public Administration, Cornell University.
21. **Directory of Consultant Members.** American Management Association. Annual.
22. **Directory of Management Consultants and Industrial Services.** Los Angeles Chamber of Commerce. Lists consulting firms, business and industrial services.
23. **Directory of Membership and Services.** Association of Consulting Management Engineers. Annual.
24. **Directory of Membership and Services.** American Management Association. Annual.
25. **Engineering Careers with Consulting Firms.** Resource Publications, D. R. Goldenson and Company. Page profiles describing the activities of the firm and the nature of engineering services, requirements for positions. Information arranged by specialty and geographic location.
26. **Industrial Research Laboratories of the U.S.** William Buchanan, ed. 5th ed. Bowker Associates.
27. **Who's Who in Consulting: A Reference Guide to Professional Personnel Engaged in Consultation of Business, Industry and Government.** Ithaca, N.Y.: Graduate School of Business and Public Administration, Cornell University.

Computer Science

28. **Index to Opportunity in Computer Sciences.** Resource Publications. Profiles of employers and details about positions available.
29. **International Directory of Computer and Information System Services.** Gale Research Company. Alphabetical listing and addresses of all types of EDP agencies.

Directories and References

30. **California International Business Directory Center for Advanced Studies in International Business.** Los Angeles. Lists California companies in alphabetical order (description, imports, exports, addresses).
31. **California Manufacturers.** Times Mirror Press. Lists California companies alphabetically, geographically, and by industry.
32. **Commercial Atlas & Marketing Guide.** Rand McNally. Lists of railroads, airlines, colleges and universities (by state). Lists of top 50 (largest) corporations: advertising agencies, commercial banks, life insurance companies, retailing companies, transportation, utilities, and industrial corporations.
33. **Current European Directories.** G. P. Henderson. Beckenham, Kent, England, CBD Research Ltd. Section 1 is an annotated guide, arranged by country in Europe, to general directories of associations, research organizations, biographical dictionaries, gazetteers, city directories. Section 2 is an alphabetical list of more specialized industry directories, incorporating title references to directories in Section 1.
34. **Dartnell Sales Manager's Handbook.** "Principal Business Directories," edited by J. C. Aspley. A list of directories, by key word, is in each edition of this handbook.
35. **Directory of Corporate Affiliates** ("Who Owns Whom"). Lists about 2,500 American parent companies with subsidiaries and affiliates. Section 2 is an index by name of subsidiary.
36. **Dun & Bradstreet, Middle Market Directory.** Lists approximately 33,000 U.S. companies with an indicated worth of $500,000 to $999,999. Gives officers, products (if manufacturer), standard industrial classification (SIC), approximate sales, and numbers of employees.
37. **Dun & Bradstreet, Million Dollar Directory.** Lists approximately 31,000 U.S. companies with an indicated worth of $1 million or over.
38. **Financial Market Place.** R. R. Bowker Company, 1972. Lists names and addresses (some foreign firms) of companies grouped by industry. Such as banks, investment organizations, capital firms, credit and collection services, stock and commodity, and so on.
39. **Funk & Scott Index of Corporations and Industries.** Lists companies by industry (names only). An index to articles on companies and industries.
40. **Guide to American Directories.** Edited by Bernard Klein. 7th ed. New York. An annotated bibliography of the major industrial, professional, and mercantile directories.
41. **Mac Rae's Blue Book.** Published annually. Several volumes of companies classified as to industry.
42. **Moody's Manuals.** Moody's Investment Sein, Inc. Has both alphabetical list

and geographical list. Has description of each company, brief history, plants, products, officers, and so on.

43. **Poor's Register of Corporations, Directories and Executives.** Alphabetical list of approximately 33,000 U.S. and Canadian corporations, giving officers, products (if manufacturer), standard industrial classification, sales range, and number of employees. The second section gives brief information on about 75,000 executives and directors.

44. **Public Affairs Information Service.** Bound volumes list selected directories under heading "Directories."

45. **Standard & Poor's Stock Reports.** Usually found in loose-leaf binder. Single page for each company listed on the New York, American, and over-the-counter stock exchanges. Each report gives fundamental position, recent developments, and so on for companies.

46. **Trade Directories of the World.** Compiled by U.H.E. Croner. New York: Croner Publications, Inc. L vol. (loose-leaf). This annotated list of business and trade directories is arranged by continent and then by country. Includes an index to "trades and professions" and a country index.

47. **Walker's Manual of Western Corporations and Securities.** M. F. Sullivan & Company. Lists corporations by city, state, and industry. A description of each is available. Aerospace, chemicals, computers, construction, merchandising, financial, food, utilities, real estate, entertainment.

48. **Who's Who in America.** Biographical data on prominent living Americans.

49. **World Who's Who in Finance and Industry.** Career sketches of leading businessmen and others noteworthy in the fields of finance and industry. A selected index by company is at front.

50. **25,000 Leading United States Corporations.** News Front. Lists top companies and industries.

Education and Teaching

51. **A Directory of Educational Programs for the Gifted.** Lavonne B. Axford. 1st ed. The Scarecrow Press, Inc.

52. **A Summary of Paraprofessional Training in Colleges and Universities.** Office of New Careers, U.S. Government Printing Office. Geographical listing of opportunities for "new careers for the poor."

53. **Accredited Institutions of Higher Education.** American Council on Education, Federation of Regional Accredited Commission of Higher Education.

54. **American Junior Colleges.** Edmund J. Gleazer, Jr., ed. 8th ed. American Council on Education.

55. **American Universities and Colleges.** Otis A. Singletary, ed. 11th ed. American Council on Education.

56. **Barron's Guide to the Two Year Colleges.** R. William Graham. Barron's Educational Series, Inc.

57. **Barron's Profiles of American Colleges.** Benjamin Fine, Barron's Educational Series, Inc. Detailed profiles on 1,350 colleges. Also, competitive ratings listed.

58. **Careers and Opportunities in Teaching.** J. I. Biegeleisen. 1st ed. E. P. Dutton and Company Inc. Considerations about teaching at various levels or

in related orientations; suggestions and list of accredited colleges with teacher education programs.

59. **Careers in Teaching and Education.** Irving Eisen. B'nai B'rith Vocational Service. Descriptions of wide variety of professional jobs of a teaching nature within the school, college, or vocational school settings.

60. **Comparative Guide to American Colleges.** James Cass and Max Biernbaum. Harper & Row Publisher, Inc. Descriptions of U.S. four-year colleges, with indexes by state, religious affiliation, selectivity, and number of degrees granted in selected fields.

61. **Comparative Guide to Two-Year Colleges and Four-Year Specialized Schools & Programs.** James Cass and Max Birnbaum. Harper and Row.

62. **Directory of National Association of Schools of Music.** National Association of Schools of Music.

63. **Directory of Accredited Institutions.** United Business Schools Associations. Alphabetical and geographic listing of accredited business schools.

64. **Directory of Accredited Private Home Study Schools.** National Home Study Council.

65. **Directory of Approved Counseling Agencies.** American Board on Counseling service, Ind., APGA.

66. **Directory of Catholic Special Facilities and Programs in the U.S. for Handicapped Children and Adults.** National Catholic Educational Association.

67. **Directory of Data Processing Education.** 2d ed. Data Processing Horizons. Lists of schools (with program descriptions) offering training programs for all phases of data processing, information on its development, the manufacturers, DP associations, publications, and training aids.

68. **Directory of Exceptional Children, A Listing of Educational and Training Facilities.** E. R. Young and Porter Sargent. 7th ed. Lists schools for private residential and day schools and treatment centers for the emotionally disturbed and socially maladjusted.

69. **Directory of Experimental Schools Issue #57.** New Schools Exchange.

70. **Directory of Free Schools.** Alternatives Foundation.

71. **Directory of Full-Year Head Start Programs.** Office of Child Development, Project Head Start, U.S. Dept. of HEW. Geographic listing with key personnel of all the programs. Addresses of regional offices.

72. **Directory of Member Colleges.** Council for the Advancement of Small Colleges.

73. **Directory of National Association of Trade and Technical Schools.** Accrediting Commission of National Association of Trade and Technical Schools. Schools listed under subject headings, alphabetical, by state, includes course descriptions and use of the school by public and private agencies.

74. **Directory of Predominately Black Colleges and Universities in the U.S.A.** National Alliance of Businessmen. Geographic directory, including enrollment, curricula, degrees offered, and description of each institution.

75. **Directory of Schools.** Stan Barondes, Dropout Center. The directory covers over 1,500 alternative and innovative schools; nationwide; K-college, and updated regularly.

76. **Directory of State and Local Resources for the Mentally Retarded.** U.S. Dept. of HEW. List of state and local agencies, facilities, and other resources which serve the mentally retarded. Includes clinical programs and

residential facilities, special rehabilitation facilities, and type of client served.

77. **The Directory of Traditional Black Colleges and Universities in U.S.** Ford Motor Company & U.S. Plywood Champion Paper Inc.

78. **Early Childhood Education Directory.** E. Robert La Crosse and R. R. Bowker. 1st ed. Guide to approximately 2,000 schools devoted to the educational interests of preschool children.

79. **Education Directory—Higher Education.** U.S. Dept. of HEW, National Center for Educational Statistics. Lists accredited institutions (alphabetical by state) in United States and its outlying areas.

80. **Education Directory—State Governments.** U.S. Dept. of HEW, Superintendent of Documents. Lists principal officers of state agencies responsible for elementary and secondary education and vocational-technical education in United States.

81. **Fourth Annual Directory of Facilities for the Learning Disabled and Catalog of Tests.** Academic Therapy Publications. Geographic listing of schools, learning centers, and clinics.

82. **Guide to Master of Arts in Teaching Program.** Anne M. Scott, State University of New York at Binghamton. Programs, by state, described by level of specialization available; program length; intern and salary information.

83. **Hand Book of Private Schools.** Porter Sargent Publications. Schools and academies listed by geographical districts; leading private schools classified; summer academic and camp programs.

84. **Index of Opportunity in the Teaching Profession.** Goldenson and Co., Inc. Employer profiles.

85. **1972 Junior College Directory.** American Association of Junior Colleges.

86. **Lovejoy's Career and Vocational School Guide.** Clarence Lovejoy, ed. Simon & Schuster, Inc. Private and public vocational school programs.

87. **Lovejoy's College Guide.** Clarence E. Lovejoy. 12th ed. Simon & Schuster. Entries for more than 3,368 American colleges, universities, junior colleges, and technical institutes; 500 programs geared to specific careers and discussion of new college board program.

88. **Private Independent Schools, The American Private Schools for Boys and Girls.** Annual. Bunting and Lyon Inc. Lists by state, summer programs.

89. **Requirements for Certification for Elementary, Secondary Schools and Junior Colleges.** Elizabeth Woellner and Maurilla Wood. 36th ed. University of Chicago Press. Listed for each state are classifications of certificates and requirements for elementary and secondary, including special subject areas, guidance, supervisory, and junior college.

90. **Scholarship Program, Education of Handicapped Children.** U.S. Office of Education.

91. **The Counselor Education Directory 1977.** Accelerated Developments, Inc. Counselor education programs; lists of institutions and the degrees, majors, and certificates available; lists 2,500 counselor educators, and state directors of counseling and guidance.

Electronics

92. **Electronic News Financial Fact Book & Directory.** Annual. Lists officers and directors, products, and sales for electronic companies.

Entertainment

93. **Celebrity Service International Contact Book.** Earl Blackwell. International trade directory of the entertainment industry. Lists names, addresses, and telephone numbers in New York, Hollywood, London, Paris, and Rome. Stage, screen, radio, TV, dance, music agents.

94. **Ross Reports Television: New York Casting, National Script Contracts.** Television index, monthly. For New York, lists advertising agencies, TV commercial producers, TV talent agents, script agents, independent firm studios. For West Coast, includes script markets, film studios, and casting.

Engineering

95. **Index of Opportunity for Engineers.** Resource publications. Engineering employers including industrial and government agencies. Descriptions of types of positions offered and the requirements for each.

96. **Index of Opportunity for Engineers Series.** Resource publications. A series of 10 volumes arranged geographically.

Food Processing and Distributing

97. **Frozen Food Fact Book & Directory.** National Frozen Food Association. Lists members of association by state. Lists are broken down into several different divisions (packers, brokers, warehouses).

98. **Grocery Distribution Guide.** Greenwich, Conn.: Metro Market Studies, Inc. Grocers listed by city and state.

99. **Supermarket Grocery and Convenience Store Chains.** Business Guides Inc. Lists of supermarkets by city and state.

100. **Thomas Grocery Register.** New York: Thomas Publishing Company. Lists: Supermarket chains by states; exporters, importers, brokers; canners; frozen foods; packers; warehouse; trade associations.

Foundations

101. **The Foundation Directory.** New York: Russell Sage Foundation. Listings of over 5,000 foundations including general purpose and activities.

Government

102. **A Directory of Public Management Organizations.** U.S. Government Printing Office. National organizations of state and local governments and associations of public officials with an interest in public employee-management relations.

103. **Directory of Government Agencies.** Libraries Unlimited, Inc. Lists department and description.

104. **Directory of Urban Corps Programs.** National Development Office. Alphabetical and state listing of urban corps programs.

105. **U.S. Government Organizational Manual.** Office of Federal Register, General Services Administration. Annual. Contains a description and organization

chart for all government agencies and departments with the names of the principal officers in each.

Health Services

106. **Directory of Member Services.** American Association of Psychiatric Services for Children. Geographic directory including names of key personnel, listing of approved training centers and programs in career child psychiatry.

107. **Health Organizations of the United States and Canada.** Ithaca: Graduate School of Business and Public Administration, Cornell University. Lists national, regional, and state organizations involved with health and related fields in the United States and Canada.

108. **Hospitals.** Guide issue of the *Journal of the American Hospital Association,* Parts 1 and 2. Chicago: American Hospital Association. Lists hospitals.

Home Economists

109. **Directory of Home Economists in Business.** St. Louis: American Home Economics Association.

Hotel and Travel

110. **Hotel and Motel Redbook.** American Hotel Association Directory Corporation. Annual. Complete listings of all hotels and motels in the United States and selected list for other parts of the world. Includes addresses, name of manager, cost of accommodations, and so on.

111. **Hotel and Travel Index.** Hollywood, California: Elwood M. Ingledue. Lists over 7,000 hotels and resorts throughout the world, travel agents, and other travel information.

Insurance

112. **Best's Digest of Insurance Stocks.** A. M. Best Company.

113. **Best's Life Insurance Reports.** A. M. Best Company.

International Business

114. **American Agencies Interested in International Affairs.** New York: Council on International Affairs. Lists approximately 300 organizations; gives the names of officers, purposes, founding dates, and other pertinent data.

115. **American Register of Exporters and Importers, Inc.** American Register of Exporters/Importers Corporation. Directory of over 30,000 manufacturers, export/import buying agencies, by product class. Also foreign offices of chamber of commerce and U.S. buying agencies.

116. **Bureau of International Commerce Trade Lists** (of every country). United States Department of Commerce. Annual. Lists American firms, subsidiaries, and affiliates in country with brief descriptions and address.

117. **Directory of American Business in Germany.** 6th ed. Seibt-Verlag. Alphabetical listing of the German companies and their American counterparts;

alphabetical listing of companies in the United States with their counterparts in Germany.

118. **Directory of American Firms Operating in Foreign Countries.** Compiled by J. L. Angel. 7th ed. New York World Trade Academy Press. Section 1 lists companies alphabetically, giving name of officer in charge of foreign operations, and countries of operation; Section 2 lists companies by county of operation; Section 3 classifies the firms by product or industry.

119. **Directory of Foreign Firms Operating in the United States.** J. L. Angel. Directory, World Trade Academy. Simon & Schuster, Inc. Lists American companies that are affiliated or divisions of foreign countries.

120. **Directory of International Engineering and Construction Services.** National Construction Association. Information about each member company in the association and description of their particular interests in the construction industry.

121. **Directory of Opportunities for Graduates.** Cornmarket Press Ltd., Annually in October. Reference book for undergraduates and their advisers for work in Great Britain.

122. **Directory of Overseas Summer Jobs.** National Directory Service, Charles James, ed. Vocation-work.

123. **Directory of United States Firms Operating in Latin America.** Pan American Union. Company listings (including the name of each manager) arranged by country.

124. **Federal Jobs Overseas.** Pamphlet #29. U.S. Civil Service Commission. Describes overseas jobs in nine departments of the federal government. Included are Departments of Agriculture, Air Force, Army, Navy, Commerce, Interior, State, and the Agency for International Development, Panama Canal Company, Peace Corps, and the U.S. Information Agency.

125. **Foreign Affairs Research, Directory of.** United States, Bureau of Intelligence and Research. U.S. university affiliated centers whose main purpose is social science research in foreign affairs. Includes focus, research projects, and publications of each.

126. **Guide to British Employers.** Cornmarket Press Ltd. Annually in October. Editorial articles written specially for professional executives and technical staff; 160 major employers in Britain; new developments of company, salary, and project information.

127. **Guide to Foreign Information Sources.** Semiannual. Washington, D.C.: Chamber of Commerce of the United States of America. Contains sources of information on foreign nations, addresses of foreign embassies, organizations and services offering information, and annotated bibliography.

128. **How to Get the Job You Want Overseas.** Arthur Liebers. Pilot Books. Tells you where the jobs are, who is offering them, as well as salary scales and employment benefits. Covers private industry and government opportunities.

129. **International Almanac of Business and Finance.** *Finance* magazine. Annual. A list by country, of U.S. corporations operating in that country, of U.S. banks, leading banks of the country, and of U.S. brokerage firms. Gives address and name of manager.

130. **Jacger's Europa-Register: Teleurope.** Darmstadt, Deutscher Adressbach-Verlag. Address of European firms, in two parts: alphabetical list by country; classified trades section.

131. **Rand McNally International Bankers Directory.** Annual. Officers, directors, and balance sheet data for United States and principal foreign banks.

132. **Social Work Opportunities Abroad.** New York: National Association of Social Workers. A directory of over 100 organizations offering social work opportunities in foreign countries. Identifies the type of social work engaged in by the organization.

133. **Trade Directories of the World.** Compiled by U.H.E. Croner. New York: Croner Publications, Inc. 1 vol. This annotated list of business and trade directories is arranged by continent and then by country. Includes an index to "trades and professions" and a country index.

134. **U.S. Non-Profit Organizations in Development Assistance Abroad.** Technical Assistance Information Clearing House. Comprehensive directory of information on over 400 non-profit organizations, agencies, missions, and foundations and their work in 124 countries in Africa, East Asia and Pacific, Latin America, and Near East-South Asia. Alphabetical listing giving programs and objectives with cross-reference by region, country, and organization.

135. **U.S. Voluntary Organizations and World Affairs.** Center for War/Peace Studies, vol. 11-intercom. Listings of national organizations and community organizations concerned with world affairs, explaining their purposes and activities, addresses, and size of staff.

136. **Who Owns Whom: International Subsidiaries of U.S. Companies.** London: O. W. Roskill. A directory of U.S. parent companies with names of their subsidiary and associated companies outside the United States. Companion volumes by this same publisher are **Who Owns Whom:** (Continental Edition), 2 volumes, and **Who Owns Whom: U.K. Edition.**

Investments

137. **The Blue Book.** Investment Bankers Association of America. Directory of U.S. and Canadian member firms of the association, arranged geographically. Includes officers and nature of business conducted.

138. **Investment Companies** (includes mutual funds). Wiesenburger Services, Inc. Lists description of background and management policy of investment firms.

139. **Money Market Directory.** New York: Money Market Directories. A directory of 4,600 institutional investors and their portfolio managers. Includes assets for each. Part 1 covers "Tax-Exempt Funds" (pension funds, endowments, foundations); Part 2, "Investment Services" (banks, insurance, investments, services, Canadian and foreign operations). Both are listed geographically with alphabetical indexes.

140. **Security Dealers of North America.** Geographical directory of U.S. and Canadian firms, with alphabetical index. Provides names of officers and partners; nature of business conducted.

Library and Information Science

141. **American Library Directory.** Helaine MacKeigan. 31st ed. R. R. Bowker Company. Biennally. Lists public libraries, county and regional systems, college and university libraries, and private libraries. Information includes names of key personnel and addresses.

142. **Directory of Library Consultants.** John Berry, III. R. R. Bowker. Lists qualified consultants in the United States and Canada and in every area of librarianship. Names, addresses, backgrounds. Listed alphabetically and by specialty.

143. **Directory of Special Libraries and Information Centers.** Anthony Kruzas. Gale Research. Volume I lists information facilities in the United States and Canada. Special libraries in colleges and universities, branches of public library concentrating on one group of subjects, company, government, and non-profit-sponsored libraries; volume II, geographic and personnel listings.

144. **Index of Opportunity in Library and Information Science.** Resource Publications. Page profiles of employers. Cross-indexed by geographic areas.

Lists of Companies

145. **Advertising Agencies Ranked by Billings.** A ranking of advertising agencies appears in the February issue of *Advertising Age* magazine each year.

146. **Annual Report of Housing Giants.** A listing published each year in the July issue of *Professional Builder* magazine.

147: **Electronics. Top 100.** A listing published each year in the July issue of *Electronics News* magazine.

148. **The Fortune Directory.** A comprehensive list of major companies; the lists appear in issues of *Fortune* magazine each year.
    a. 500 largest U.S. industrial corporations, largest banks, merchandising, transportation, life insurance, and utilities (May issue).
    b. Second 500 largest U.S. industrial corporations (June issue).
    c. 200 largest foreign industrial corporations, 50 largest foreign banks (August issue).

149. **Major Independent Finance Companies.** A listing published each year in the April issue of *Bankers Monthly* magazine.

150. **The 500 Largest Corporations.** A listing published each year in the May issue of *Forbes* magazine.

Marketing Research

151. **Bradford's Directory of Marketing Research Agencies in the United States and the World.** 13th ed. New Rochelle, New York: Ernest S. Branford.

Manufacturers

152. **Directory of Key Plants.** Market Statistics, Inc., 2 volumes. A directory of 41,000 plants with 100 or more employees. Volume I is by state and county and within each county, by SIC and employment size; Volume II is by SIC and then by state and county.

153. **Kelley's Manufacturers and Merchants Directory.** 2 volumes, annual. World directory of merchants and manufacturers with comprehensive coverage for British Isles, and sections listing companies by major product for other countries. Includes a "Trades & Services Index."

154. **Thomas Register of American Manufacturers.** 10 volumes, annual. Volumes 1–6 list manufacturers by specific product; Volume 7 is alphabetical list of companies, giving address, branch offices, subsidiaries, products, estimated capitalization, and occasionally, principal officers. Volume 8 is "Index" to product classifications and includes a list of leading trade names (pink), boards of trade, chambers of commerce. Volumes 9–10 are "Catalogs of Companies."

Merchandising

155. Retailer Owned Cooperative Chains; Wholesale Grocers; Wholesaler Sponsored Voluntary Chains. Business Guides, Inc. Lists companies by country and state.

156. Shopping Center Directory (United States and Canada). National Research Bureau, Inc. Lists shopping centers by city and state.

Petroleum

157. Appraisal Survey, Petroleum Industry. John S. Herold, Inc. Appraisal reports for more than 100 oil and gas companies.

Professional Associations

158. Directory of Historical Agencies in the United States and Canada. Biennial. Madison: American Association for State and Local History. Lists historical commissions, departments of archives and history, state and local historical associations, historical libraries, and other resources in this field.

159. Directory of National Trade and Professional Associations of the United States. Washington, D.C.: Columbia Books, Inc. Alphabetical list of 4,300 national trade and professional associations, with key word and Executive indexes. Gives chief officer, number of members, annual budget, publications.

160. Encyclopedia of Associations. Volume 1: National Organizations of the U.S. 13th ed. Detroit: Gale Research Company. A comprehensive list of all types of national associations, arranged by broad classifications, and with an alphabetical and key word index. Gives name of chief officer, brief statement of activities, number of members, names of publications, and so on.

Public Utilities

161. Moody's Public Utility Manual. Moody's Investors Service, Inc. Alphabetical list of utilities including information on companies.

162. Public Utilities Information Sources. J. E. Hurst. Gale Research Company. Bibliography and directory of electric, gas, telephone, and water industries.

Publishing

163. American Book Trade Directory. Helaine MacKeigan. 24th ed. R. R. Bowker Company. Directory of bookstores in the United States and Canada, arranged geographically by state and city, lists 10,000 U.S. and 600 Canadian book outlets in 2,500 cities with a guide to the type of stock carried.

164. Ayer Directory; Newspapers, Magazines and Trade Publications. Philadelphia: N. W. Ayer & Son, Inc. Firm, newspaper advertising agents.

165. Ayer's Directory of Newspapers and Periodicals. Philadelphia: N. W. Ayer & Son, Inc.

166. Directory of Scholarly & Research Publishing Opportunities. Academic Media. Lists magazines and other publishing concerns by subject category.

167. Editor and Publisher International Year Book. Editor and Publisher. Encyclopedia of the newspaper industry. Directory of over 8,000 U.S. and Cana-

dian weekly and nondaily newspapers. Directory of newspapers in Latin America, Europe, Asia, Africa, and Australia. Lists major U.S. and Canadian advertising agencies responsible for newspaper advertising.

168. **Literary Market Place.** The Business Directory of American Book Publishers. J. A. Neal. 38th ed. R. R. Bowker Company. Annual. Facts on 22,000 firms and individuals in U.S. publishing—list names, titles, addresses, phone numbers.

169. **Names and Numbers.** 21st ed. R. R. Bowker Company. Provides an alphabetical index to over 17,000 names of publishers with phone number, street address, city, zone. Companion to *Literary Market Place*.

170. **Newspaper International.** National Register Publishing Company. Lists newspapers and newsweeklies in over 90 countries. Published annually in January, plus updating supplements.

171. **Publisher's International Directory.** 7th ed. R. R. Bowker Company. Directory gives names and addresses of 20,000 active publishers in 144 countries.

172. **Standard Periodical Directory.** Annual. A subject listing of 53,000 U.S. and Canadian periodicals, giving address, scope, year founded, frequency, subscription rate, circulation, and one basic advertising rate. Alphabetical index at end.

173. **Who's Who in Publishing—An International Biographical Guide.** 2d ed. R. R. Bowker Company. Contains detailed biographical data of 3,500 leading persons in the publishing field.

174. **Writer's Market.** Annual. Cincinnati: F. & W. Publishing Corporation. Lists over 3,000 possible markets for writers, photographers, and artists. Requirements and other pertinent information are included.

Public Relations

175. **Professional Guide to Public Relations.** Richard Weiner. Prentice Hall. Lists 500 PR services with names, addresses, phone numbers of firms, and key personnel. Services include: clipping bureaus; literary; mailing, radio, and TV. PR services; media directories, motion picture distributors; fine art and rare photo services.

Research Centers and Laboratories

176. **American Council of Independent Laboratories Directory.** American Council of Independent Laboratories, Inc. An alphabetical guide to the leading independent testing, research, and inspection laboratories of America. Has cross-references by services offered and geographic location of the laboratory.

177. **Directory of American Council of Independent Laboratories.** Washington, D.C.: American Council of Independent Laboratories. Listing of laboratories; information on activities and senior scientific personnel. Revised.

178. **Directory of Federal R & D Installations.** National Science Foundation. A listing of 700 federally owned and directly controlled R & D activities, providing information on their location, size, funding, and major functions and activities.

179. **Directory of Scientific Resources in the Washington, D.C. Area.** Washington, D.C. Lists research and development organizations, social and psychological

science groups, documentation, operations, research and computer specialists, and federal government laboratories.

180. **Directory of University Research Bureaus and Institutes.** 1st ed. Detroit: Gale Research Company. Lists research and development organizations, social and psychological science groups, documentation, operations research and computer specialists, and federal government laboratories.

181. **Directory of Urban Affairs Information and Research Centers.** Eric V. Winston. Scarecrow Press. Alphabetical and geographical listing of organizations including purposes, activities, director, size of staff, and areas of concern.

182. **Governmental Research Association Directory.** Biennial. New York: Governmental Research Association. Lists over 1,000 individuals and organizations professionally engaged in doing research for federal governmental agencies.

183. **Industrial Research Laboratories, of the United States.** 15th ed. Edited by Jacques Cattell Press. New York: R. R. Bowker Company. Information on 5,000 nongovernmental laboratories devoted to fundamental and applied research, and operated by 3,000 organizations, industrial firms.

184. **List of Concerns Interested in Performing Research and Development.** Annual. Washington, D.C.: Small Business Administration. Lists approximately 3,000 small firms doing research and development work in a variety of categories. Entries include the research or development in which firms specialize.

185. **Research Centers Directory.** 5th ed. Detroit: Gale Research Company. A directory of 4,500 research institutes, centers, foundations, laboratories, bureaus, and other nonprofit research facilities in the United States and Canada. Information includes scope of research activities and names of publications.

Social Service

186. **Community Action Agency Atlas.** Office of Economic Opportunity. Geographic listing of all agency offices, regional, state, local, and those in Indian land areas.

187. **Conservation Directory.** National Wildlife Federation. Annual. Governmental and private organizations concerned with natural resource use and management.

188. **Directory of Agencies Serving Blind Persons.** American Foundation for the Blind. Revised biennially. Lists 500 American agencies and schools serving blind.

189. **Directory of Approved Counseling Agencies.** American Board on Counseling Services Inc., American Personnel and Guidance Association. Directory of counseling agencies which have been evaluated and approved. Includes sponsor, clientele, fees, and professional staff. Arranged geographically for the United States and Canada.

190. **Directory of Full Year Head Start Programs.** Office of Child Development, HEW. Geographic listing of the programs including the names of the directors.

191. **Directory of Positions.** Sociocom, monthly. Lists positions in social and economic development field. Divided by job category and sublisted by state.

192. **Directory of Spanish Speaking Community Organizations.** U.S. Government Printing Office. Listing of national, state, and city organizations.

193. **Directory of State and Local Resources for the Mentally Retarded.** U.S. Department of HEW. List of state and local agencies, facilities, and other resources which render services to the mentally retarded.

194. **Directory—United Way of America.** United Way of America. Listing of United Funds, Community Chests, and Community Health and Welfare Councils which are members of United Way of America. Address and name of executive included.

195. **JWB Personnel Reporter.** National Jewish Welfare Board. Biannual. Listing of current job openings in Jewish community centers and other personnel and training information.

196. **Public Welfare Directory.** American Public Welfare Association. Lists all federal, state, local, and territorial public welfare agencies throughout the United States and Canada. Lists other related public agencies—federal and state level.

Appendix B

Personal inventory

1. Identification

Name _____

Address _____

_____

Home telephone _____ Business telephone _____
                      (area code)   (area code)

2. Education

a. Degree
(list most recent degree first)	Date completed	Major	School	Grade point average
_____	_____	_____	_____	_____
_____	_____	_____	_____	_____
_____	_____	_____	_____	_____
_____	_____	_____	_____	_____

196

b. Name of courses taken in area of emphasis; also, courses relevant to career interest.

_____

_____

_____

_____

c. Special projects, term papers, research studies.

_____

_____

_____

_____

d. Other professional training including: company sponsored training programs, correspondence courses, or specialized education and duration of each.

Course name	Date
_____	____ to ____
_____	____ to ____
_____	____ to ____
_____	____ to ____

e. Honors, fellowships, scholarships, and other awards due to scholastic achievement.

_____

_____

_____

_____

f. Functions which you are capable of performing **as a result of formal education.** Start with the function in which you possess highest proficiency; be specific.

_____

_____

_____

_____

_____

_____

_____

_____

_____

_____

3. Work Experience
(Repeat #3 for every full-time position held.)

Company: _____

Department: _____

Location: _____

Dates of employment: _____

Supervisor's name: _____

Answer the following questions by giving the following information: What exactly did you do? What were the circumstances? Were you solely responsible or part of a team? What were the benefits to the company, to other employees, and to you?

a. State your direct job responsibilities and describe the activities performed to do your job.

_____

_____

_____

_____

_____

_____

_____

_____

b. Were your efforts instrumental in company cost reduction?

_____

_____

_____

c. Did you stimulate additional sales or identify new markets?

_____

_____

_____

d. Were you responsible for enlarging the current line of products or services?

_____

_____

_____

_____

e. Were you responsible for improvements by redefining job functions within the company?

_____

_____

_____

_____

f. Did you improve company operations by installing new systems or procedures?

_____

_____

_____

_____

g. What circumstances surrounded your promotions?

_____

_____

_____

_____

h. What contributions have you made to your department, to its operation, to the employee morale?

_____

_____

_____

_____   _____

i. Were you responsible for identifying new company policies, directions, or objectives?

_____

_____

_____

_____

j. Were you awarded recognition or honors for works within your industry?

_____

_____

_____

_____

4. Summer or Part-time Jobs:

Dates	Job function	Hours/Week
_____ to _____	_____	_____
_____ to _____	_____	_____
_____ to _____	_____	_____
_____ to _____	_____	_____

Special achievements:

_____

_____

_____

_____

5. Military Service

Present status _____

Branch of service _____

Rank at entrance _____

Rank at discharge _____

Special assignments and achievements:

_____

_____

_____

_____

_____

_____

_____

6. Extracurricular Activities

Activities while enrolled in school (e.g., service clubs, athletic teams, academic organizations, social clubs.) List committee memberships, offices held, contributions, and improvements achieved.

Activities other than school activities (e.g., political and civic affiliations, professional societies, club memberships, hobbies, avocations). List committee memberships, offices held, contributions, and improvements achieved.

---

7. References

a. Name —————————————————————————

Position or title —————————————————————

Organization or college ————————————————

Address ————————————————————————

Telephone ( ) ——————————————————————
        area code

b. Name ————————————————————————————

Position or title ——————————————————————

Organization or college ————————————————

Address ——————————————————————————

——————————————————————————————————

Telephone (   ) ———————————————————————
          area code

c. Name ————————————————————————————

Position or title ——————————————————————

Organization or college ————————————————

Address ——————————————————————————

——————————————————————————————————

Telephone (__) ———————————————————————
          area code

Appendix C

Employer data form

1. What is the job description? What are the responsibilities?

   _____

   _____

   _____

   _____

   _____

   _____

2. What functions will the employee be required to perform in carrying out the responsibilities?

   _____

   _____

   _____

   _____

   _____

   _____

3. What additional skills will be required to qualify for promotion after successful completion of assignments?

_____

_____

_____

_____

_____

_____

4. What college degrees and other educational preparation is required to qualify for the position?

_____

_____

_____

_____

_____

5. Is work experience required? What kind? How much?

_____

_____

_____

_____

_____

_____

6. Are extracurricular activities and achievements weighted in evaluating qualifications?

_____

_____

_____

_____

_____

_____

7. Is military service record considered?

_____

_____

_____

_____

_____

8. What career direction would be preferred in a candidate for the position?

_____

_____

_____

_____

_____

9. What personality characteristics are preferred?

_____

_____

_____

_____

_____

_____

10. What personal motivational factors are desired in a prime candidate?

_____

_____

_____

_____

_____

_____

Appendix D

Qualification ranking

Employee selection criteria	My qualifications
1.	1.
2.	2.
3.	3.
4.	4.
5.	5.
6.	6.
7.	7.
8.	8.
9.	9.
10.	10.

Index